the Business of Adventure

Developing a Business in Adventure Tourism

K. ROSS CLOUTIER

DEPARTMENT CHAIR, ADVENTURE PROGRAMS DEPARTMENT

UNIVERSITY COLLEGE OF THE CARIBOO

Copyright 1998
Bhudak Consultants
#171—230—1210 Summit Drive
Kamloops, British Columbia V2C 6M1

Cover photograph: Pat Morrow
Copy Editing: Anne Ryall
Layout and Design: digital banff graphic arts
Printed in Canada by Hignell Book Printing, Winnipeg

Canadian Cataloguing in Publication Data

Cloutier, K. Ross, 1956-
   The Business of Adventure

Includes bibliographical references and index.
   ISBN 0-0682474-0-7

1. Tourist trade. 2. New business enterprises. I. Title.
G155.C2C5682 1997   910'.68   C97-910653-2

Introduction

This text is intended as a resource for both students and business owners involved in adventure tourism. It is compiled from selected instructional materials used in courses taught by the author to outdoor guides and aspiring adventure business owners. As such, it presents specific business topics as applied to the adventure industry and does not represent a comprehensive text on all aspects of either business or adventure.

There is little doubt that the last decade has seen enormous growth and interest in the commercialization of adventure sports. The efforts expended by a whole generation of outdoor recreationists to have their high-risk endeavours become widely recognized, economically viable and socially acceptable activities have resulted in the completely new service industry of adventure tourism. As a consequence we are now seeing a vast amount of interest from other, more non-traditional users of the globe's wilderness regions.

One of the signs of the maturation of a new business sector is the development of a supporting and interpretive body of literature. As adventure sports evolve from what has historically been seen by much of North American society as anti-establishment behaviour (a perception encouraged by many participants) to a more mainstream, significant economic generator, this supporting literature will develop as well. This text is just one step in the long evolution of such material.

Acknowledgements

I am grateful to Anne Ryall for her editing assistance, Geoff Powter for the design of the book and advice and Pat and Baiba Morrow for supplying photos. Thanks are also due to Naomi Cloutier, Jim Everard, Greg Foweraker, Iain Stewart-Patterson, Kathy Richardson, Neil Hartling and Dave Stark for their assistance, input and advice.

Contents

Chapter One ❖ The Adventure Industry

The Roots of Commercial Adventure 10
Self-esteem and Value-forming Experiences 12
The Tourism - Personal Growth - Recreation Cycle 13
The Size of the Industry..15

Chapter Two ❖ Business and Guiding

A Case Study 22
Guiding and Business Efficiencies 24
The Guiding Mosaic 25
The Business Mosaic 26
Profit Margins, Equity and Risk...28
Starting a Business 30
Barriers and Profitability...31

Chapter Three ❖ Forms of Business Organization

Proprietorship...36
General Partnership 37
Limited Partnership 37
Corporation 38
Cooperative 39
Non-profit Society...39
Appendix: Partnership Agreement 40

Chapter Four ❖ Business Finance and the Adventure Industry

Current Asset Management 46
Short-term Financing 47
Long-term Financing 48
Income Statements 50
Balance Sheets 51
Bottom-up Budgeting 54
Ratio Analysis 55
Financial Analysis of Private Companies.................................57

Chapter Five ❖ Stages of Business Growth

Inception and Incubation 62
Development and Survival 62
Growth 63
Expansion and Maturity 64

Chapter Six ❖ Business Plan Development

Requirements of the Business Plan 68
The Executive Summary 68
The Company 69
The Product or Service 69
The Market 69
Competition 70
Sales and Marketing 70
Operations 70
Financial 71

Chapter Seven ❖ Start-up Action Plans

Mission Statement 74
Personal Strengths and Weaknesses 74
Investment Risk and Return 75
Lifestyle Goals 75
Capital Sources and Investment Types 75
Pricing Strategy 76
Credit 76
Corporate Structure 76
Corporate Values and Ethics 76
Management Considerations 77
Business Risk 77

Chapter Eight ❖ Adventure Product Development

Characteristics of Adventure Tourism 80
Positioning Adventure Products 80
Product Positioning Maps 81
Distribution Channels 84
Operator Restrictions and Wholesale Markets 85
Pricing Adventure Products 86
Break-even Analysis 87
Establishing Prices with a Bottom-up Approach 89
Profit Margins 90
Marketing Expenditures 92

Appendix ✦ Sample Business Plan

The Executive Summary *96*

Company Overview
Origins 99
Mission Statement 99
Objectives..99
Current Status 99

Organization of Company
Legal and Financial Status 100
Share Structure 100
Management 100
Roles 100
Role Descriptions..101
Personnel Policies 101
Contractors 101

Strategy for the Future ....
Where Is the Company Going? 101
Company Strategy...102

The Product
Product Description...103
Positioning 103
Market Needs for the Product 104

The Market
Market Statistics 105
    Size of the Market 105
    Rate of Growth 106
    Purchasing Characteristics 107
Company Perspective on the Market................107
    Product Line 107
    Market Trends 108
Reaction to the Market......................................109
    Introduction Difficulties 109

Competition

Overview 109

Competition Prices 110

Adventure Company Pricing 111

Sales and Marketing

Advertising and Promotion.................................111

Strategies for Introduction 112

Company Operations

Product Packaging 113

    Facilities 113

    Equipment 113

    Trip Preparation 114

    Qualified Staff 114

Financial Forecast

Financial Assumptions 115

Pro Forma Balance Sheet - January 1996 116

Pro Forma Income Statement...............................117

Pro Forma Balance Sheet - December 1996 118

Break-even Chart 119

Condensed Income Statement 119

Financial Analysis 120

Cash Flow Statements 121

Trip Pricing Assumptions 123

Start-up Expenditures 124

Loan Assumptions 125

Attachments..126

Index 131

Chapter One

The Adventure Industry

No longer content to snap photos from a crowded beach, more tourists are trading in their suntans and shorts for equipment that will allow them to participate in adventure sport activities. Over the last decade, adventure sports have made significant inroads towards becoming socially acceptable, mainstream activities in which status-conscious travellers participate. Once the domain of alternative-lifestyle youth with no discretionary income, active outdoor recreation is worth almost 50 percent of the $400-billion U.S. travel industry today.

The industry appeals to more than death-defying risk-takers and is now driven by families, travellers over fifty, collectors of kudos, upper-income earners, women and young children. Adventure has been made easier and sometimes even safer in order to bring it within reach of the general traveller.

As an economic driver, the adventure industry has become a cornerstone within many local and national economies. In the United States, over 13,000 outdoor sporting goods stores and 9,000 specialty stores support this industry. In Canada, the four Mountain Equipment Co-op stores alone grossed over $93 million in 1995. A study completed by the Province of British Columbia in 1994 estimated that total expenditures for outdoor recreation on B.C. Crown lands were nearly $4 billion per year, with B.C. residents accounting for about 80 percent of that spending. There is no longer any doubt: adventure is big business.

An avalanche starts slowly: as a hidden layer, a slow rumbling, a roar. It builds to a huge moving mass until, suddenly, it's everywhere. A global trend starts the same way. It is nothing, unheard of — then it is everywhere. So, too, is the trend to adventure. Once a misunderstood alternative lifestyle, it is now a major economic driver in the global tourism economy.

> *"But if adventure has a final and all-embracing motive, it is surely this: we go out because it is in our nature to go out, to climb the mountains and to sail the seas, to fly the planets and to plunge into the depths of the ocean. By doing these things we may touch with something outside or behind, which strangely seems to approve our doing them. We extend our horizon, we expand our being, we revel in a mastery of ourselves which gives an impression, mainly illusory, that we are masters of our world. In a word, we are men and women, and when we cease to do these things, we are no longer."*
>
> ❖ Wilfred Noyce

The Roots of Commercial Adventure in Canada

The opening of the Canadian Pacific Railway in 1885 provided access to the Rocky Mountain and Selkirk ranges and, in turn, necessitated the recovery of the construction cost of the railway itself. The CPR recognized the potential ability of tourism to contribute to the payment of this debt and went to great lengths to advertise in the eastern United States and in European cities for tourists to travel to the "Canadian Alps". In order to facilitate the experiences of these tourists, the CPR constructed extravagant facilities such as Glacier House at Rogers Pass, the Chateau Lake Louise and the Banff Springs Hotel. The development of support services such as horse outfitters and trail guides was encouraged in order to provide activities and services for the tourists.

By 1899, the CPR had brought its first Swiss mountain guides to Canada with the intent of providing full-fledged mountain-guiding services from Glacier House at Rogers Pass. Commercial adventure tourism had begun, and it was helping to pay for a railroad.

Table 1-1 ✦ Mountain Guiding Development in Canada

1871	CPR survey begins
1883	CPR begins advertising for tourists
1884	Banff Springs Hotel and Glacier House built
1885	CPR completed on November 7th
1897	First Swiss mountain guide in Canada: Peter Sarbach
1899	First Swiss mountain guides brought to Canada by the CPR
1901	First ascent of Mount Assiniboine
1902	First ascent of Mounts Bryce and Columbia
1909	Conrad Kain brought to Canada by the Alpine Club of Canada
1913	First ascent of Mount Robson by Conrad Kain
1920	Glacier House closed in mid-1920s
1950	Only Ernst and Edward Fuez guiding in the Lake Louise area
1955	Only four mountain guides active in Canada
1957	Four additional mountain guides licensed in Canada
1957	Heli-skiing started in Canada by Canadian Mountain Holidays
1963	Association of Canadian Mountain Guides (ACMG) formed
1966	First ACMG guide's course held with four candidates
1968	First ACMG assistant guide's course held
1972	ACMG accepted into the International Federation of Mountain Guides
1976	Forty European mountain guides working in Canada
1990	ACMG training program redesigned into Ski Guide, Alpine Guide and Rock Guide streams
1991	First edition of ACMG training manual completed
1993	First paid ACMG Technical Director hired
1996	University College of the Cariboo assists with the ACMG Training and Certification Program registration and administration

Source: ACMG Technical & Professional Guidelines, *1996*

Outward Bound: Self-esteem and Value-forming Experiences

The inspiration behind Outward Bound Schools came from the German-born educator, Kurt Hahn. Hahn was born to parents of Jewish descent in 1886. In World War I he was assigned to the German Foreign Office and at the end of the war became private secretary to Prince Max of Baden. In 1920, Prince Max constructed a wing onto his castle for a school and called it Salem. The philosophy of the school was less concerned with academic achievement than with student attitudes, ambitions and perceptions. Hahn perceived youth to be surrounded by the "decay of care and skill, the lack of enterprise and adventure, and the loss of compassion". In addition to academics, his pupils were challenged by the physical stresses of athletics, by the exercise of patience in the task of craftsmanship and by expeditions on land and water.

In 1932, Hahn came out publicly against Hitler. In 1933, he was arrested and imprisoned but was released through the influence of highly placed friends. Exiled from Germany, he founded Gordonstoun School in Scotland. At Gordonstoun, Hahn added seamanship to the curriculum because he felt it necessary to introduce youth to danger and adventure in order to create a learning environment that would provide "the moral equivalent of war". Hahn never advocated adventure for its own sake, but rather as a training tool through which youth would mature.

With Gordonstoun founded and accepted among the British educational elite, Hahn sought to extend his ideas to other educational institutions. In order to establish his curriculum ideas around adventure, resourcefulness, community service and the use of expeditions, he developed a syllabus of activities that could be used by other educators. His aim was to "impel young people into value-forming experiences... an enterprising curiosity, an undefeatable spirit, tenacity in pursuit, readiness for sensible self-denial, and, above all, compassion". This was to become the basis for Outward Bound School philosophy and curriculum.

In the summer of 1941, after the start of the war, the first Outward Bound School was founded in Aberdovey, Wales. While many of the students were young seamen, others were apprentices sent by industry, police and fire agencies, or were about to go into the armed services.

In 1962, the Colorado Outward Bound School became the first Outward Bound School opened in the United States. This was soon followed by the Minnesota school in 1964 and the Hurricane Island, Maine, school in 1965.

In 1966, a group formed in Vancouver, British Columbia, which was to become Outward Bound Canada. Keremeos, B.C., was selected as the site for the first Canadian school, and in June 1969, 30 students attended the first Canadian Outward Bound Mountain School course. Three 26-day courses for boys aged 16 to 19 were offered that summer. In 1975, the Canadian Outward Bound Wilderness School, located north of Thunder Bay, Ontario, began independent from the Mountain School. Outward Bound presently operates approximately 30 schools in 25 different countries.

Table 1-2 ❖ Yamnuska Inc.

Yamnuska Inc. started as an adult "wilderness program" at the Rocky Mountain YMCA's Yamnuska Centre in the late 1970s. Programs included backpacking, rock climbing and mountaineering. Gaining momentum, the Wilderness Program left the YMCA, and Yamnuska Mountain School, a non-profit society directed by Bruce Elkin, was formed and based in Bruce's basement in Canmore, Alberta. The years following saw a steady evolution as instruction in mountaineering and in rock and ice climbing became the core activity and the fall Mountain Skills Semester an annual event. By the early 1980s, Yamnuska Mountain School was at the apex of the instructional market.

By 1984, Yamnuska had become Yamnuska Mountain School Ltd., owned by James Blench and Marnie Virtue. In 1983, David Begg emigrated to Canada from New Zealand and started a small Ottawa-based guiding company called Greater Heights Mountain Adventures which ran climbing courses in the East and summer mountaineering programs in Europe and the Rockies. In September 1988, the assets of Yamnuska Mountain School Ltd. were purchased by David, and Greater Heights was named Yamnuska Inc.

Source: Yamnuska Inc. Guide Handbook

The Tourism - Personal Growth - Recreation Cycle

Commercial adventure sport activities in Canada began primarily through the CPR-initiated trail- and mountain-guiding activities near the turn of the century. These activities generated significant visitor numbers as well as revenue for both western Canada and the railway. It can be seen from Table 1-1 that during and after the Great Depression and the Second World War the number of commercially guided clients participating in mountaineering activities dropped to the point where in the 1950s there were only two active mountain guides in the Banff region. This was due to a number of primary factors: a lack of interest; a lack of available disposable income on the part of foreign tourists and Canadians during the Depression and the war years; and the self-reliant, non-outdoor-recreationist mentality of resident Canadians, who did not view the resources of Canada as a playground during these years, but rather as a source of extractable wealth to raise themselves — and their country — back onto a solid economic footing.

The 1960s brought a new stage for much of the travelling public. Personal and national wealth grew significantly throughout most of the Western world, air travel became increasingly affordable for many, and leisure time and disposable income rose dramatically. Recreational activities began to boom during the 1960s and 1970s as they became less exclusive and more affordable to the middle classes. Municipal recreation departments and YMCAs began to program outdoor recreation activities, churches offered summer youth camp programs, universities and colleges increased their physical education and recreation program enrolments, and private companies began to offer outdoor instructional courses.

By the mid-1970s, government departments had begun to give legitimacy in a roundabout way to adventure activities through their application of Kurt Hahn-style educational theories to therapeutic adventure programs for young offenders. Working at government-funded, therapy-based outdoor programs such as DARE in Ontario, Enviros in Alberta, Camp Trapping in British Columbia, or other such programs, became a well-paying method for skilled outdoor adventurers to support their recreational pursuits while at the same time developing personal experience and skill levels for future endeavours within the industry.

The late 1970s and early 1980s saw the formation of many private adventure-related companies due to an evolution of market demand and an interest in the development of personal skill-mastery courses. On the one hand, this was not a drive towards tourism per se, but a demand for personal skills that would enable the course participant to develop and master a particular adventure sport, and in turn carry out his or her own activities in a safe and competent manner. Course leaders played the role of instructor rather than guide, and there was little interest on the part of the instructor or course participant in either a guided trip or a facilitated, therapeutic experience.

However, there was also an ever-increasing demand from a select clientele that the industry provide the means to experience the wilderness environment for those who had neither the time nor the desire to develop the personal expertise required to carry out the activities on their own. Companies within the heli-ski, trail riding, hunting and rafting sectors were early to develop this potential and provide the value-added services that this clientele demanded. This fast-growing product became the initial driving force behind the industry we recognize today as adventure tourism.

The fact that the primary focus for most adventure activities in Canada started with a tourism service philosophy in the last century, that it has evolved through therapy and skill mastery focuses as primary stages of employment, and that it is now back within a framework of global tourism, has been lost on much of the industry. Organizations struggling to maintain a "previous stage" philosophy within the quickly evolving adventure industry have experienced both financial and philosophical growing pains by not recognizing or responding adequately to changing trends and market demands.

There are many examples of how this previous-stage mentality has caused turmoil within an organization. The Canadian and United States Outward Bound Schools have long struggled with whether to exclusively offer what tend to be money-losing "personal growth" courses based upon the early philosophy of the organization or to balance these with the lucrative and more market-driven "professional development" programs which do not meet the original start-up philosophy of either Kurt Hahn or the individual school. A similar example is the post-secondary institution whose recreation or physical education degree was developed in the 1970s and is not applicable to today's student or employer because the curriculum has not changed significantly; as a result the institution graduates students without current knowledge or credentials for working in today's industry.

Figure 1-1 ✧ The Tourism - Personal Growth - Recreation Cycle

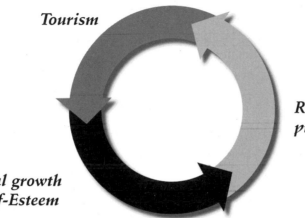

Tourism

Recreation and pursuit of skills

Personal growth and self-Esteem

The Size of the Industry

Attempting to put a finger on the actual size of the outdoor recreation industry has been futile at best. The varying interpretations of which activities should be included, along with the difficulty of capturing data from the small "mom and pop" businesses, have made the creation of a definitive study very difficult. Those studies which have been carried out tend to be incomplete and inconsistent. Although there are numerous sources of information which provide data on the size of the industry within Canada, two recent studies serve in providing partial estimates of the economic impact of commercial outdoor recreation in British Columbia.

The first of these studies that is of interest is the *Forest, Range and Recreation Resource Analysis,* completed in 1994 by the British Columbia Ministry of Forests. The Ministry's interest in the scale and scope of outdoor recreation stems from the fact that it is responsible for managing outdoor recreation on approximately 85 percent of the province's lands — which is most of the Crown land outside of parks.

According to this study, nearly 60 percent of all outdoor recreation use on B.C. Crown land occurs in provincial forests, and about 40 percent occurs in national, provincial and regional parks. Total actual expenditures for outdoor recreation on Crown land are estimated to be nearly $4 billion per year, with B.C. residents accounting for about 80 percent of those expenditures. Annual net economic value of outdoor recreation on Crown land is estimated to be nearly $1.5 billion, with B.C. residents accounting for about 74 percent of this value. The estimated $780 million in non-resident outdoor recreation expenditures on B.C. Crown land represents about 30 percent of all reported non-resident tourism expenditures.

Figure 1-2 ❖ Tourism and Outdoor Recreation Expenditures in B.C. (1993)

(in millions of 1993 CAN$)

Type of Use	B.C. Residents	Non-residents	Total
Tourism	3,000	2,700	5,700
Outdoor recreation on Crown land	3,130	780	3,910
Total tourism and outdoor recreation	5,380	2,720	8,100

The second study of interest, which was completed in 1996 by Price Waterhouse and the ARA Consulting Group for the British Columbia Ministry of Tourism and the Council of Tourism Associations of B.C., is the Tourism Growth Management Strategy. A portion of this study concentrated on calculating the size of "outdoor tourism" products within the B.C. tourism industry (as of 1994) as well as making projections of industry growth to 1999.

This study included the following activities in its definition of "outdoor tourism products": hiking/backpacking, wildlife viewing, whitewater/sea kayaking, canoeing, rafting, power/sail boating, scuba diving, trail riding, bicycling, hunting, snowmobiling, ski touring and climbing.

Figure 1-3 estimates the number of companies which specialize in outdoor activities but are not accommodation-based. This list is incomplete since there is no accurate inventory or consistent capacity measure for these companies at this time.[1]

Table 1-3 ❖ Definitions Used by the Ministry of Forests

In its 1994 study, *Forest, Range and Recreation Resource Analysis*, the British Columbia Ministry of Forests created some interesting distinctions between outdoor recreation and tourism use:

> Tourism and outdoor recreation, though frequently mentioned together, are not synonymous. Tourism use refers to overnight use, by both B.C. residents and non-residents, for both outdoor recreation and non-outdoor recreation motives. It excludes day-use recreation, which is a significant activity by B.C. residents. Outdoor recreation use refers to both day and overnight outdoor recreation use by B.C. residents and non-residents. Tourism includes some outdoor recreation. Outdoor recreation includes some tourism, but excludes non-outdoor recreation tourism use such as visiting friends and family, or business trips.
>
> *Source:* Forest, Range and Recreation Resource Analysis, *p. 239*

Table 1-4 ❖ Definitions Used by the Tourism Growth Management Strategy

O utdoor tourism products provide the traveller the opportunity to enjoy the outdoor setting. The traveller may participate in an outdoor activity or may choose to just relax and enjoy the setting.... Outdoor experiences can be undertaken independently or provided by a tourism business which may offer guides, equipment, transportation, accommodation and meals".

"This product can be divided into two major groups. The first group is comprised of companies which provide services for individuals to take part in outdoor activities, but do not offer fixed-roof accommodation. The second offers accommodation facilities where outdoor activities are staged from the facility."

Source: B.C. Tourism Growth Management Strategy, *p. B4-1*

Figure 1-3 ❖ The Number of Outdoor Operators in British Columbia without Accommodation

Water-related

Power/Sail cruising...168
Wildlife viewing 50
Scuba diving 69
Kayaking 57
River rafting 50

Land-related

Trail riding 52
Hut-to-hut 23
Guide outfitters 255
Bike/Hike 45
Heli-ski/Snowcat[2] 24
Others...23
Companies with multiple activities 36
Companies with activities unknown..............36

Total businesses 897

1 *These are British Columbia-based companies only. Any estimate of the number of operators in B.C. would need to take into account non-B.C.-based companies that use part of the province for their operations. A good example are the numerous Banff/Canmore, Alberta-based guiding companies which use B.C. for their programming yet may not be counted here as B.C. operations.*

2 *Heli-ski/Snowcat operations were not included in "outdoor activities" in the study since they were classified as "ski product".*

Accommodation facilities which provide accommodation for outdoor activities are listed in the following table and include both room and campsite accommodation.

Figure 1-4 ❖ The Number of Outdoor Operators in British Columbia with Accommodation[3]

Number of lodges	573
Number of lodge units	8,668
Number of campground sites	11,695

The following table provides an estimate by the Growth Management Strategy of revenues for outdoor activities in 1994. These estimates include both non-accommodation- and accommodation-based companies.

Figure 1-5 ❖ Revenue Estimate for Outdoor Activities in British Columbia in 1994

Water-related	*$million*
Power/Sail cruising	34
Wildlife viewing	9
Scuba diving	12
Kayaking	9
River rafting	11
Subtotal	*$75*
Land-related	
Trail riding	9
Hut-to-hut	6
Guide outfitters	26
Heli-ski/Snowcat	65
Other outdoor companies	16
Subtotal	*$122*
Other	
Hunting by residents	125
Provincial Parks	388
Outdoor accommodation	168
Subtotal	*$651*
Total revenue	*$848*

[3] *This figure does not include provincial or national park campground revenues*

The Fashion, Leisure and Household Products Branch of Industry Canada gathers statistics on the retail sale of outdoor clothing and equipment in Canada. Statistics in the recent "Canadian Outdoor-market Survey" show that, of all outdoor-related clothing and equipment sold in Canada, 33.8% is clothing, 26.1% is equipment, 22.2% is footwear, 13.8% are accessories and 4.1% are other outdoor-related items. Table 1-5 shows the total sales by category for 1994.

Table 1-5 ❖ Retail Sales of Outdoor Clothing and Equipment in Canada

Item	Total Sales (millions of 1994 CAN$)
Canoes	30
Kayaks	8
Personal watercraft	100
Bikes and accessories	440
Camping equipment	163
Fishing and hunting equipment	270
Ski and snowboarding equipment	130
Mountain-climbing equipment	4
Water-sports equipment	40
Rugged outdoor footwear	250
Ski boots	40
Total	**$1,475,000,000**

Notes:

1. *Camping equipment includes: backpacks, sleeping bags, camp stoves, tents, etc.*
2. *Water-sports equipment includes: SCUBA/skin-diving equipment, water skis, windsurf boards, life jackets, etc.*
3. *At least one third of bikes sold are other than mountain bikes.*
4. *The total excludes outdoor clothing.*

References

Canadian Outward Bound Wilderness School. *The Instructor's Handbook*. 2nd ed. 1986.

Klassen, K. *Association of Canadian Mountain Guides: Technical and Professional Guidelines*. 2nd ed. 1996.

Miner, J., and J. Boldt. *Outward Bound USA*. William Morrow and Company, 1981.

Ministry of Forests. *Forest, Range and Recreation Resource Analysis; Economic Analysis of Timber, Range and Recreation Resources*. 1995.

North Carolina Outward Bound School. *The Instructor's Handbook.* 4th ed. 1986.

Price Waterhouse, and ARA Consulting Group Inc. *Tourism Industry Product Overview: Towards a Tourism Growth Management Strategy*. 1996.

Yamnuska Inc. *Company Guidelines*. 1991.

Chapter Two

Business and Guiding

*M*ark Wilson's expertise as a white-water paddler was a wonder to all who watched him. As an 18-year-old who had only been paddling for three years, his proficiency was as much a result of natural talent as it was of good instruction from his friends. Mark had recently graduated from high school in 1972 with a high school diploma and advice from his school counsellor to pursue a career which would pay well and would let him pursue his paddling interests as leisure. The counsellor suggested becoming a school teacher because, from what he knew, nobody made a living from paddling. Although Mark saw this as well-meaning advice, he could not envision himself at an indoor job; even though his parents didn't understand what the program was all about, he enrolled that fall in an outdoor recreation degree program at the nearby university.

Courses in the outdoor recreation degree emphasized that society's leisure time was increasing dramatically and that recreation programmers should understand that recreation was a higher-level need described within Maslow's hierarchy which played an important role in its application to special populations such as seniors, the disabled and young offenders. Mark was encouraged to become a generalist and took multi-disciplinary courses in psychology, sociology, criminology, geography, administration, parks planning and recreation programming as well as outdoor recreation activities such as backpacking and canoeing. He felt that the program was all right but did not give him any additional "hard skills", focusing more on the "touchy-feely" aspects of using outdoor recreation for facilitating group interaction, personal growth and self-esteem.

Mark was pleasantly surprised when, during the summers while he was at university, he was offered work doing outdoor trips at a group home for young offenders. The intent of the trips was to "provide recreational opportunities for the youth and to use the outdoors to model and explore alternative behaviours". There was talk of helping the youth "bridge" their outdoor experiences back to their home environments, although exactly how to do this was a little vague. One thing was for certain: Mark was logging hundreds of days of backpacking and canoeing trips — which was all that really mattered to him. He was the envy of all his friends who were working at construction and railroad jobs to pay for their next year's schooling.

After completing his degree in 1976, Mark heard of a new, year-round camp that was being started in the province to run therapeutic out-trip programs for young offenders. After taking three months off to paddle along the coast of Chile, Mark started work at this camp full time. His schedule required him to work nine months out of twelve, which left him three months to do an expedition of his own each year. He made use of his time off, with climbing trips to Mexico and Alaska, and a trek in Nepal. In the winter of 1978, he was asked to take some family friends to climb the volcanoes in Mexico, an area to which he had been the year before.

For the previous couple of years, Mark had been hearing exciting things about a new physical education degree in outdoor education at a university in another province. It was said that the focus of the program was principally on the development of hard skills, and this certainly fit in well with what he knew was the emphasis of physical education degrees. When he checked into the program, he was enthused to find an emphasis on performance development, training theory, anatomy, physiology and kinesiology. Most important to Mark was the program's focus on the development of technical proficiency in white-water paddling, rock climbing, mountaineering and skiing. As it would only take him two additional years to get this degree, he enrolled in the fall of 1980.

Once in the outdoor education degree program, he found that a good deal of emphasis was on how to use the outdoor sports within the school system as a physical education teacher, and how to present the sports to others by using correct instructional techniques, analysing the students' movement skills and applying proper training régimes.

During his two winters in this program, Mark taught kayak rolling sessions in the pool and instructed cross-country skiing for the local ski club. After he graduated in 1982, he spent a number of summers instructing rock climbing to young adults for the local YMCA camp, which had just begun an instructional climbing program. He found it a little strange to be told by the camp director not to get involved in how the group he was teaching functioned: they were paying only to be taught the skills and not to be "told how to behave by some granola-chewing hippie". This was all right with Mark since he didn't take personal offense, and it certainly made his job less demanding. During the winters he continued to work for a variety of therapeutic programs for young offenders.

It was while he was working at the YMCA that two significant things happened to Mark. The first was when he was hired and told that he was a contractor, not an employee of the camp. He didn't know exactly what this meant, except that the camp did not take off as many deductions as had other places he had worked, and this left him with more money each month. He decided to ask his friend Greg Cuthbertson, who was an accountant, about this someday soon.

The second significant thing that occurred was that during August of 1985 four of the participants on an advanced rock-climbing course asked him if he would take them on a trip to ski around Mount Logan in the Yukon. They had heard that the trip was possible but had no idea how to plan it; and anyway, they wanted an expert skier along in case of an emergency. Mark agreed to undertake the planning, to provide the food and group equipment necessary, and to act as the trip guide. A date was set for the next spring, a fee was agreed to for these services, and Mark found himself preoccupied with planning the trip.

It was January 1986, and Mark had just arrived home from two months spent trekking in Nepal, when he received a call from some acquaintances in California. Would Mark guide them on a one-week ski-touring trip somewhere in the Canadian Rockies in April? They also had other groups of friends who would like to do a similar trip. Why not? He had skied the Wapta Traverse on his Ski Guide's course the previous spring, and it would be a logical trip since it had huts that could be used. Before he was off the phone, he had filled three weeks of trips.

Mark knew he had entered a new stage of his career. Without any real effort on his part he had filled nearly two months of the year with guiding work, some of which would let him travel to areas he had not yet been to. What would happen if he sold trips actively? He already had lots of contacts from his 10 years of work in the field. He also had numerous ideas for trips that could be sold: sea kayaking in British Columbia, Baja and Chile; mountaineering trips in Mexico, Alaska and the Yukon; trekking trips in Nepal; hut-to-hut hiking trips in Europe; ski-touring trips in the Rockies — and what about building a hut himself? Now he wished he knew something about running his own business and how to market...

Just as Mark was about to find out, adventure tourism has its roots in lifestyle skills but its future in the application of business technique. There has been tremendous recognition within the guiding and tourism industries over the last decade of the potential profit in adventure sport activities. The application of good business management principles is no longer thought of as unnecessary, but as a crucial element to ensure a financially rewarding living from a lifestyle of adventure.

Many long-time guides have sacrificed a large portion of their skiing or paddling time to the challenge of company start-ups and the pursuit of computer skills, marketing ability, personnel management or internet web-page development as ways to improve their potential to make a living from the industry. Their personal contacts from many years of working within the field form the basis for business start-ups, marketing contacts, training programs, and contract or consulting work. Entrepreneurial initiative and business skills have become important components to blend with kinetic skills and trip experience in order for an adventure to be a success.

Guiding and Business Efficiencies

Individuals have historically been drawn to work within the various adventure activities because of a primary interest in an outdoor, travel-oriented lifestyle. This emphasis upon the lifestyle and recreational interests of the individuals involved has led to an underdeveloped industry. The industry has also been constrained by the unique and specialized nature of the activities, the perceived unacceptability of the activities by much of mainstream society, and the transient, alternative-lifestyle orientation of many of its participants.

Most past and present adventure businesses have been started by these "lifestyle" operators. With the relatively recent identification of the marketability and profit potential of commercialized adventure activities by business owners and investors, there has been much interest on the part of these players to integrate business management techniques with the sports. The industry is seeing tourism development investors actively seeking viable operations in which to invest or purchase.

Figure 2-1 shows a visual interpretation of both efficient and inefficient weighting in the balance between sport/guiding knowledge and business knowledge. Efficient weighting would do a better job of facilitating the development of the industry as a whole, and would better enable guides to make a suitable living.

Figure 2-1 ❖ A Balance of Lifestyle and Business

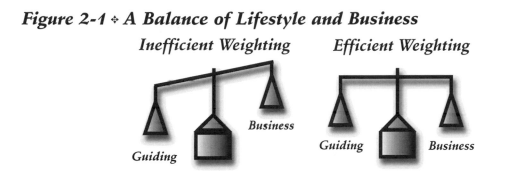

The Guiding Mosaic

The leading of groups into the wilderness environment requires a broad range of skills and expertise on the part of guides. Figure 2-2 demonstrates the types of skills that guides need to acquire in order to competently lead commercial groups. The diagram clearly shows the integrated nature of the knowledge, skills and abilities of five primary task areas: *interpersonal, safety, technique, environment* and *culture*.

Figure 2-2 ❖ The Guiding Mosaic

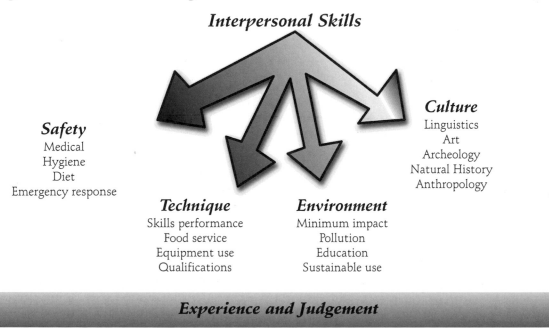

The possession of an engaging personality and good *interpersonal skills* is paramount for leaders who are involved in working with both individuals and groups in instructional situations which can sometimes be long and stressful.

Safety refers to the all-encompassing nature of the guide's role in keeping guests healthy and safe with respect to hazards brought about by being in the wilderness. This includes aspects of hygiene, diet, medical care, search and rescue, and the management of emergencies.

Technique refers to the requirement for a guide to be a highly skilled expert in the primary activity undertaken, along with the secondary and tertiary activities such as equipment use, equipment care and food preparation. There is an expectation that the guide will have skills and background knowledge which far surpass the functioning levels of trip participants.

Environmental knowledge refers to the guide's ability to impart to guests a respect for and an understanding of the natural resources the adventure industry depends upon. This may include techniques of minimum-impact camping, educating guests as to pollution and litter control, or educating local residents in a Third World culture with respect to environmental stewardship. The larger picture may include teaching guests about land use preservation or zoning issues in order to protect the natural resource base for future generations to use.

Culture refers both to aspects of foreign culture and to the local heritage. Guides who are leading groups to foreign countries are obliged to have a good understanding of the local language, art, archaeology, natural history and anthropology. Part of the ability to add value to a guest's trip is to assist with the interpretation of the local culture and its people. Guides who are leading foreign clientele on local trips also have an obligation to interpret the heritage, history and natural history. In most cases, people travel to other cultures, or others travel to ours, to explore and understand the diversity and differences between the two.

The underlying principle behind the development of good guides is the necessity for broad experience levels and good judgment. It has been said that good judgment is the result of bad experience, and it is exactly this principle that is shown as the underlying aspect of guiding. It is imperative — regardless of a guide's academic background or industry qualifications — that the experience level be broad, and judgment in both relaxed or stressful times be accurate.

The Business Mosaic

The identification of necessary business skills is sometimes hard for the guide who is in transition towards being a business owner. The tendency is to improvise as issues come up and to learn on the job. Figure 2-3 shows a schematic of a number of the major knowledge areas that business owners need to acquire in order to operate effectively. Just as in adventure activities an individual may have more aptitude and interest in one sport than in another, so too in business activities individuals may have more aptitude or interest in marketing than accounting, or in administration than staff management.

The underlying characteristic of most adventure businesses is that their owners are attempting to craft a living from the adventure activities and the environment they love;

however, the very nature of a business requires that it remain viable by being profitable from year to year. Without this viability the owners cannot maintain their offering of programs to the public, and there will be no employment of guiding or support staff by the business. The risk associated with investment in the highly speculative adventure industry (when there are many other more conservative investment opportunities available) dictates that the investor must receive a fair return.

Figure 2-3 ✦ The Business Mosaic

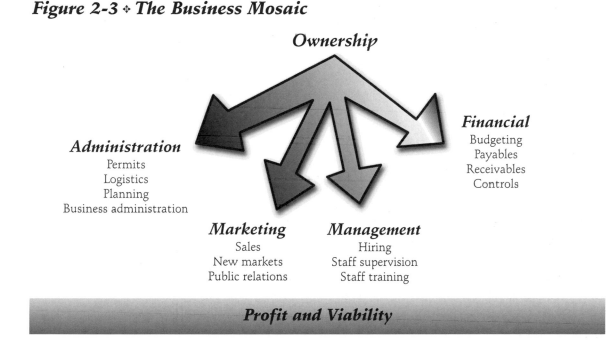

Marketing skills refer to the ability to identify new clientele, to clearly communicate the products offered to the customers, to price and sell the product, and to maintain a positive product and company image in the public eye.

Administration skills refer to the logistical, planning and administrative actions necessary for the business to operate. This may include permits, insurance, correspondence, filing, scheduling and other administrative functions.

Management skills refer to the management of office and guiding staff, in-house training requirements, safety controls and other management functions which will make the business function effectively.

Financial skills refer to the planning and management of budgets, the management of money coming in and going out of the business, the allocation of financial resources to other elements such as marketing, and the application of suitable financial controls to meet financial projections.

Profit Margins, Equity and Risk

By 1990, Mark Wilson had built Elias Guiding to the point where it ran hiking and rock climbing trips in the summer, ski-touring trips in the winter, and the occasional ski or mountaineering expedition in the spring. The business employed three or four guides who were contracted as necessary to run the trips. It had grossed $100,000 in revenue during the 1989 year. Mark was happy with how things had evolved over the previous few years. However, he was disturbed that he had spent so much time over the last five years on the business and had so little to show for it financially. He was considering what to do about this.

Mark met with his accountant, Greg, who then organized the business' cash flow for 1989 by activity. This format is presented in Table 2-1.

Table 2-1 ❖ Elias Guiding: Cash Flows, 1989

Revenue

Hiking trips	20,000
Rock-climbing trips	24,000
Ski-touring trips	56,000
Total revenue	**$100,000**

Expense

Equipment purchase	4,500
Food for trips	12,000
Guide contracts	35,000
Hotel & hut accommodation	18,000
Insurance	2,000
Marketing	10,000
Supplies	5,000
Vehicle costs	13,000
Total expense	**$99,500**

Net cash inflow **$500**

Mark felt better when Greg explained to him that spending 10% of revenue for marketing in the early stages of a business was normal and that spending 40% of revenue on wages was considered low for most types of businesses. However, he was surprised that the business had spent $18,000 on hotels, lodges and backcountry huts in order to run trips for the year. He also observed that the $4,500 spent on new equipment really only maintained the $16,000 of equipment inventory the business had built up, and didn't add to the actual amount owned.

From these observations and his discussions with Greg, it was obvious to Mark that he was expending a great deal of time and energy, but the business was not building much wealth. All it really owned was about $16,000 of very used equipment and an older-model van. This was not exactly what he had in mind.

The second observation Mark made was that the business was paying a great deal of money each year — 18% of its total revenue in fact — to hotel and hut accommodation for its guests. And what were the hotels doing for it? In Mark's mind, very little. Elias Guiding spent a considerable amount of time and money marketing and selling trips to its guests, whereas the hotels, which did not contribute to this effort at all, made $18,000 a year from their efforts! Elias Guiding was taking all the marketing and business risks while other supporting businesses only had to wait for it to bring guests through the door for them.

To make things worse, Greg also explained to Mark that industry-wide hotel profit margins averaged 70% for their rooms, 30% for beverage service and 10% for food service. He compared this to the 0.5% net cash inflow that Elias Guiding had made in 1989 on its operations.

All of a sudden it became clear to Mark what the solution was. A number of his friends were building their own backcountry lodges. They were attempting to keep the potential profits from all possible sectors: 70% for providing overnight accommodation and 10–30% for providing food and beverage services. This, along with what would be left from running the actual trips, would allow their businesses to be far more profitable than his. Also, the amount saved by not paying the other support businesses would easily pay for the construction and financing of his own building.

The other, longer-term benefit that Greg explained to Mark was that of acquiring equity. The construction of an accommodation facility would help the business to acquire a sellable asset, one that would appreciate in value over time as opposed to losing its value like the type of equipment the business owned at present. This interested Mark a great deal.

This concept of "vertical integration" has been extremely common within the adventure industry during the 1990s for two primary reasons. The first is simple economics: the industry-average profit margins within the accommodation sector (70%), the beverage sector (30%) and the food sector (10%) not only are higher than the profit margins from many outdoor program activities (which often average less than 10%) but also provide additional profit areas for the industry to capture.[1] The second reason that companies have been moving in this direction is illustrated in Mark's experiences: adventure businesses have realized that they are taking most of the financial and business risks while these secondary sectors benefit greatly from their efforts.

This concept of business risk has not been an important issue until relatively recent times, primarily due to the fact that investment requirements have not been large to date. However, as guests' expectations increase, business owners are continually having to invest greater amounts of money to provide better-quality facilities, equipment and services. This requires more and more inventive financing as both business owners and investors assess the amount of return possible on their capital as well as the safety of their investment. There are

---

[1] *These are industry norms for the hospitality industry.*

many demands upon investors' money; in order for the adventure industry to tap into it, returns must be reasonable and the funds protectable.[2]

Starting a Business

There is much emphasis these days upon the starting of a business as a way of entering the adventure industry. To date there is very little to stop the entry of new adventure businesses into the marketplace. The industry has been such that almost anyone with an interest in entering could do so. This has resulted in a plethora of new companies, most of which do not generate adequate revenues to last more than a few years at best, while a smaller number become successful and establish a market niche and a long-term position in the marketplace.

A second method of entering the adventure industry is to purchase an existing business. This is a business that has been developed from its inception to the point where there is something tangible to sell, either in the way of facilities and equipment, or in terms of clientele. A problem inherent in purchasing an existing business is how to value the business, as there is obvious worth in its sweat equity, assets, permits, goodwill and mailing lists — although less clear is how to assign a monetary value to each of these items.

There are obvious benefits to each method of entry. Starting a business from nothing enables a start-up group to enter the industry slowly, feeling its way along and thus determining both its own interest and that of its projected market. This is less financially committing in the early stages than purchasing an existing business, but far more uncertain as to outcome. In the long run, it is questionable whether the start-up group will save money, and if it does, this will likely be offset by the cost of labour (sweat equity). There is, however, a great deal of personal satisfaction to be gained from this approach.

Purchasing a business has the effect of shortening the cycle of business stages for the new owner (*see Chapter 5*) since the business is being bought at a more advanced stage; much of the early uncertainty has been resolved and the sweat equity required in the early stages has been contributed. Acquiring an existing company involves higher initial costs because the assets, goodwill and sweat equity are being purchased all at once. Part of the initial financial analysis required concerns whether the business cash flow can support the purchase cost. Other advantages include such things as the acquisition of permits, client lists and mailing lists, which may not be easily obtainable otherwise.

There is little doubt that the purchasing of businesses will become an increasingly important method of entering the adventure industry as influences such as the lack of land use permits and the saturation of market segments become common due to the maturation of the industry.

Table 2-2 offers an example of the valuation placed upon a backcountry lodge which was put on the real estate market in late 1994.

---

[2] *Objective investors are concerned with two primary elements: what their return on investment will be, relative to other investment options; and how safe their investment is.*

Table 2-2 ❖ The Valuation of a Backcountry Lodge, 1995

Value of license (to April 2000) $30,000
Value of buildings (lodge, sauna, shed, waste disposal) 80,000
Value of furnishings and supplies (sleeping materials, firewood, propane)....10,000
Value of business (records, mailing lists, brochures, etc.) 30,000

Total value ***$150,000***

Source: Lodge Sale Listing, ReMax Realty Multiple Listing Service, *11-22-1994*

Additional methods of business start-up include:

❖ *Joint Venture*: Allying with another company which provides working capital and access to its markets and expertise. A well-positioned partner can let you concentrate on your core expertise. The adventure industry provides many examples of successful joint ventures.

❖ *Franchising*: Buying a franchise can help you get start-up financing and minimize the risk of failure. The franchisor helps with the assembly of a business plan, accounting systems and promotion. In many ways this is similar to Outward Bound's approach, where each school operates separately from the other but uses the same marketing label and product type.

❖ *Dealership*: Allows you to purchase the right to sell another company's products, but you cannot use the company's trade name. A distributor sells to several dealers and a dealer sells to consumers or retailers. Although dealerships are used occasionally within the adventure industry for business start-ups, we are most familiar with established companies which "distribute" their product through the use of a travel wholesaler (the dealer) who sells direct to the consumer and/or through a travel agent (the retailer).

❖ *Licensing*: Licensing arrangements give you the right to operate within established guidelines. Generally, licensees can use a seller's trade name as well as specific methods, equipment, technology or products. You may pay an annual fee, a flat fee or a royalty based on sales.

Barriers and Profitability

The concept of entry and exit barriers is becoming relevant to the adventure industry as these barriers have significant effects on both the number of firms in the market place and their ultimate resale value.

Entry Barriers

A barrier to entry exists when new firms cannot enter a market in which another business is operating. Many types of barriers exist, but all have the effect of creating market power and usually increased profits for the business that is already in operation, while at the same time preventing another firm from entering the market. Examples of entry barriers include: guide qualification restrictions on the part of land managers (such as sea kayaking or climbing in the national parks); government operating regulations (such as the rafting regulations in British Columbia); exclusive permitting systems, permit quotas and/or use quotas; economies of scale (larger companies' operations may be cheaper than those of a smaller one); high up-front costs (environmental assessment reviews required by legislation or management plans, etc.); and customer loyalties.

Entry barriers have the effect of limiting the number of new companies to the industry while increasing the resale value of many businesses, because buying a business becomes a primary method of entry.

Exit Barriers

A barrier to exit exists when a firm which is in the market is prevented from leaving. Exit barriers have the effect of restricting when or how a business or shareholder may leave the market place, while lowering the resale value of the business. A good example of when the consideration of exit barriers is important is when a business shareholder wants to gauge how easy it will be to sell his or her shares for their full value when it is desired to do so.

Examples of exit barriers include: the holding of land use permits which are not transferable to a new business owner, the establishment of a business built on an individual's name and reputation rather than on a more generic trade name, short-term permit tenure which leaves uncertainty as to whether the permit will be reissued, terrain which is too technical for "tourist"-type clientele, business lawsuits that the purchaser may assume, and poor record keeping (incomplete client lists, etc.).

Barriers as Start-up Strategies

The above discussion demonstrates that entry and exit barriers need to be considered during the start-up stages of an adventure business. In many ways, they form part of a business start-up strategy; it can be seen that the higher the entry barriers to other firms the less the direct competition, and the lower the exit barriers the easier it will be to sell the business at a higher price. The reverse is also true: the lower the entry barriers the easier it will be for other businesses to enter and compete for market share, while the higher the exit barriers the harder it will be to sell and to get a good price for the business.

Thus, strategically, the best combination of business barriers is high entry barriers and low exit barriers.[3]

[3] *There is much to be said for the astute business developer who has the political awareness, diplomatic skill and patience to work through stiff entry barriers that have discouraged other operators, while structuring the business from the start so that exit is possible.*

References

Block, S., et al. **Foundations of Financial Management**. Irwin Inc., 1994.

Daft, R., and P. Fitzgerald. **Management**. 1st Canadian ed. Holt, Rinehart & Winston of Canada Ltd., 1992.

DuBrin, A., and D. Ireland. **Management and Organization**. 2nd ed. South-Western Publishing Co., 1993.

Lusztig, P., and B. Schwab. **Managerial Finance in a Canadian Setting**. 4th ed. Butterworths Ltd., 1991.

Siegel, J., et al. **Corporate Controller's Handbook of Financial Management**. Prentice Hall, 1994.

Corporation

A corporation, also known as a limited company, is a legal entity. It is recognized by the legal system as having rights and duties. An individual, a group of individuals, an incorporated organization, a group of organizations, governments, or any combination of the above many form a company for the purpose of engaging in any legal enterprise. As far as the law is concerned, a company is treated in the same way as an individual and will live until it is folded up by the subscribers, the courts or the Registrar of Companies. A corporation can own property, can be sued (or sue) and files income tax returns.

A company may divide its assets and liabilities as it chooses; it can establish any lines of authority it likes; it can require any level or type of investment of its members, including none. Unless its memorandum or by-laws state otherwise, it can engage in any kind of business it likes, raise funds where it wishes, and pay dividends or otherwise dispose of its assets as it pleases. Voting rights and therefore direction of the firm are proportional to the amount of voting shares held. The risk of the shareholders is limited to the amount of money they have invested, unless they have voluntarily taken on greater liability, such as by signing a personal guarantee.

Shares in the company may be distributed in a variety of different formats, including voting and non-voting, common and preferred. Moreover, shareholders are often designated as having rights of membership on the board of directors or may even be prohibited from sitting on the board. Where there is an option for "preferred" shares, they carry no rights of decision making but guarantee the holder a preferred position whenever dividends are declared. In a small corporation the shareholders, directors and officers may be the same people.

Incorporation procedures are relatively complex and are more expensive than for any other legal form. Some tax advantages occur, particularly where there will be substantial capital assets. At dissolution, remaining assets are distributed according to the shares held. Typically, the firm will also have a shareholders' agreement drawn up and registered.

There are two general types of corporation: *private* and *public*. The public corporation offers its shares for sale to the general public once its prospectus meets with the approval of regulatory agencies. The shares are generally traded on a stock exchange and can be bought and sold at will — subject to their availability. There are no limits on the number of shareholders. In a private corporation, the transfer of shares is usually restricted by its articles to approval by the board of directors or other shareholders.

A company can incorporate either federally or provincially. If a business will be operating primarily in a single province it usually incorporates provincially. The provincial incorporation allows the company to carry on business in other provinces, but its head office must stay in the incorporation province. The federally incorporated business can locate its head office in any province, although it must register in each province in which it is carrying on its business.

Advantages of incorporating include:

❖ **Limited Liability** The shareholders of a corporation are liable only for the amount they have paid for their shares. If the corporation goes bankrupt, creditors are not able to sue its shareholders for its debts.

❖ **Ownership Transfer** If shareholders want to sell their interest in the company, they have only to sell their shares. In a private corporation, this sale may require the approval of the board of directors; a shareholders' agreement is important to clarify the terms under which shares may be sold.

❖ **Contracting with the Corporation** A shareholder can sue or contract with the corporation.

❖ **Raising Capital** Corporations, by offering shares for sale, can raise required capital for expansion or operation (this assumes there is a market for the shares).

❖ **Taxation** In some cases, there may be tax advantages for a business to be incorporated.

Co-operative

A co-operative is a form of association in which all members have exactly equal say in the direction of the co-operative's activities: one person equals one vote, even if the level of investment is not equal. The co-operative is operated for the purpose of providing its own members with goods or services. Its surplus revenue is returned to its membership in the form of patronage refunds.

Non-profit Society

While one seldom sees a non-profit society doing significant levels of business under its own incorporation, it is not prohibited by law from doing so, providing any "business" activities are not its principal reasons for existence. Non-profit does not mean that the society may not have a surplus of revenues over expenditures, only that it may not distribute such surpluses to its members or officers. However, if a society consistently engages in profit-making activities, Revenue Canada may deem it to be a taxable body.

Usually, a non-profit society that wishes to engage in business will incorporate a wholly owned or shared-ownership subsidiary company. The company may then be deemed to be taxable unless the parent society is registered as a tax-receipt-granting body, in which case the surpluses of the company may be donated to the society in exchange for a receipt.

Appendix 3-1❖ Sample Partnership Agreement

PARTNERSHIP AGREEMENT

This partnership agreement is made in _____ (number) original copies between:

(1) _____ (partner)

(2) _____ (partner)

(3) _____ (partner)

(the "Partners").

1.0 PARTNERSHIP NAME AND BUSINESS

1.01 The Partners agree to carry on a business of _____ _____ (type of business) as partners under the business name _____ (the "Partnership").

No person may be added as a Partner and no other business may be carried on by the Partnership without the consent in writing of all the Partners.

1.02 The principal place of business of the Partnership is _____ _____ _____ (address).

2.0 TERM

2.01 The Partnership begins on _____ (date) and continues until terminated in accordance with this agreement.

3.0 PARTNERSHIP SHARES AND CAPITAL

3.01 The Partners shall participate in the assets, liabilities, profits and losses of the Partnership in the percentages beside their respective names ("Partnership Share"):

_____   _____ % /100

_____   _____ % /100

_____   _____ % /100

3.02 The Partners shall contribute a total of $ _____ in cash, in proportion to their respective Partnership Shares, to the start-up capital of the Partnership by no later than _____ (date).

3.03 If further capital is required to carry on the Partnership business, the Partners shall contribute it as required in proportion to their respective Partnership Shares.

3.04 No interest accrues on a Partner's capital contribution to the Partnership Share.

4.0 BANKING AND FINANCIAL RECORDS

4.01 The Partners shall maintain a bank account in the name of the Partnership business on which cheques may be drawn only on the signature of at least _____ (number) of the Partners.

4.02 The Partners shall at all times maintain full and proper accounts of the Partnership business each is involved in, and these accounts shall be accessible to each of the Partners on reasonable notice.

5.0 PARTNERS' ACCOUNTS AND SALARIES

5.01 The financial records of the Partnership shall include separate income and capital accounts for each Partner.

5.02 No Partner shall receive a salary for services rendered to the Partnership, but the profit or loss of the Partnership shall periodically be allocated to the Partners' separate accounts in order for the Partner to access the funds in this account.

5.03 The capital accounts of the Partners shall be kept in proportion to each of their respective Partnership Shares.

5.04 No Partner shall draw down his or her capital account without the previous consent in writing of the other Partners.

6.0 MANAGEMENT OF PARTNERSHIP BUSINESS

6.01 Each Partner may take part in the management of the Partnership business.

6.02 Any difference arising in the course of carrying on the Partnership business shall be decided by the Partners having a majority of the Partnership Shares.

7.0 PARTNERS' DUTIES

7.01 Each Partner shall at all times duly and punctually pay and discharge his separate debts and liabilities and shall save harmless the property of the Partnership and the other Partners from those debts and liabilities and, if necessary, shall indemnify the other Partners for their share of any payment of his separate debts and liabilities by the Partnership.

7.02 No Partner shall assign or encumber his share or interest in the Partnership without the previous consent in writing of the other Partners.

7.03 No Partner shall bind the Partnership or the other Partners for anything without the previous consent of the other Partners.

8.0 YEAR-END

8.01 The fiscal year-end of the Partnership shall be _____ (month and day) in each year.

9.0 TERMINATION OF THE PARTNERSHIP

9.01 The Partnership may be dissolved at any time during the lives of the Partners by a Partner giving notice in writing to the other Partners of his intention to dissolve the Partnership. In such a case, the Partnership shall be dissolved on the date stated in the notice.

9.02 The Partnership is dissolved on the death or insolvency of any of the Partners.

9.03 On dissolution of the Partnership, subject to any contrary agreement binding the Partners and their estates, the Partnership business shall promptly be liquidated and applied in the following order:
   a) to pay the debts and liabilities of the Partnership,
   b) to refund any outstanding additional advances,
   c) to the distribution of the credit balances in the Partners' separate income accounts,
   d) to the distribution of the credit balances of the Partners' capital accounts,
   e) to the distribution of any residue to the Partners in proportion to their respective Partnership Shares.

10.0 DISPUTES

10.01 Any dispute between the Partners arising out of or related to this agreement, whether before or after the dissolution of the Partnership, shall be referred to and settled by a single arbitrator agreed upon by the Partners. The decision of the arbitrator is final and binding on the Partners, with no right of appeal.

11.0 MISCELLANEOUS

11.01 The terms of this agreement may only be amended in writing dated and signed by all Partners.

11.02 This agreement binds the Partners and their respective heirs, executors, administrators, personal representatives, successors and assigns.

11.03 This agreement is governed by the laws of the Province of
_____ (province).

11.04 If any provision or part of any provision in this agreement is void for any reason, it shall be removed without affecting the validity of the remainder of this agreement.

This agreement is executed on _____ (date).

Signed, sealed and delivered)
in the presence of:)
)
_____)   _____ (partner name)
)
_____)   _____ (partner name)

_____)   _____ (partner name)
(witnesses)

References

Block, S., et al. **Foundations of Financial Management**. 3rd Canadian ed. Irwin Inc., 1994.

Lusztig, P., and B. Schwab. **Managerial Finance in a Canadian Setting**. 4th ed. Butterworths Ltd., 1991.

Ministry of Economic Development of British Columbia. **Licensing and Regulations for B.C. Business**.

T he management of finances within a business is critical to the success of any firm, including firms in the adventure industry, where financial management is playing a larger and larger role in the viability of companies. As the adventure industry raises expectations and becomes more professional, and as companies become larger and more global, the financial officer of the company must manage the finances of not only local but also international operations. An understanding of finance is also critical to business owners who must determine how to finance the start-up or expansion of their dreams. Decision making concerning corporate strategies, investment decisions, cash flow difficulties, dividend payments, international politics and currency exchanges is becoming more and more important for adventure companies.

This chapter is intended to provide an overview of finance decision-making topics and issues as they pertain to the adventure industry. The following discussion assumes an understanding on the part of the reader of basic accounting concepts.

Current Asset Management

The financial manager must carefully allocate resources among the current assets of the company: cash, marketable securities, accounts receivable and inventory. Cash balances are largely determined by cash flowing through the company on a daily, weekly, monthly or seasonal basis as determined by the cash flow cycle. Cash flow relies on the timeliness of customer payments and the speed at which suppliers and creditors request payments. The primary consideration in managing the cash flow cycle is to ensure that the stream of revenue and expenses within a business is properly synchronized.

Figure 4-1 shows the cash flow cycle. The sale of an adventure service produces either a cash sale or an account receivable (on credit) which will be collected some time in the future. When the account receivable is collected it becomes cash. By providing customers with credit (accounts receivable) one is making it easier for them to purchase the service (which is positive) while at the same time reducing the amount of cash on hand (which is negative). This credit may be provided by offering 30, 60 or 90 days for them to pay, requiring only a deposit at the point of sale and allowing the remainder of the fee to be paid later, or by allowing customers to purchase with short-term financing techniques such as credit cards. Decisions must be made thoughtfully regarding accounts receivable policy, recognizing that it is a two-edged sword; on the one hand it facilitates the sale, while on the other there is an opportunity cost to the business in not having the cash on hand immediately to invest or to pay for operating needs.[1]

---

[1] *Generally, many adventure businesses could make better use of a well-thought-out credit policy in order to better facilitate (and assist the customer in self-financing) the sale, while at the same time doing a better job of investing cash in short-term, liquid, marketable securities (GICs, T-Bills, etc.). A decision such as not allowing customers to pay with credit cards is, in essence, a decision to not allow the customer to self-finance the purchase, and has the result of forcing the purchaser to pay cash for the entire cost of the trip all at once.*

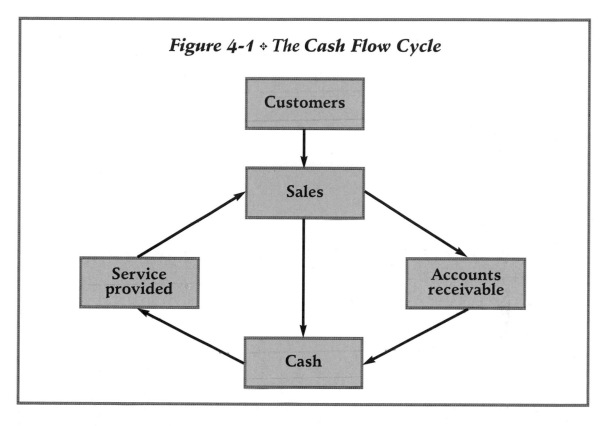

Figure 4-1 ❖ The Cash Flow Cycle

Financing

Business managers access sources of funds that are external to the company when cash flows are inadequate for certain needs. Short-term funds are generally used in order to finance current operating expenses and temporary current assets, while long-term funds are used to finance more permanent fixed assets. A business requires access to capital for start-up costs, the purchase of fixed assets, operating costs and, ultimately, for expansion purposes. The business manager's choice of financing sources is one of the most important business decisions that will be made. Appropriate financing requires the forecasting and planning of future capital needs in order to have suitable access to funds for the business. It must also minimize the cost of these funds as much as possible. The issues become those of appropriate timing as well as affordability.

Short-term Financing

Short-term funds are those which generally need to be paid in less than one year; they might include credit cards, bank credit and credit from suppliers. The seasonal operating cycles that force adventure companies to incur highly fluctuating operating costs make it necessary to obtain various forms of short-term credit. Many small businesses do not have access to long-term capital and are forced to rely heavily on short-term bank and trade credit. This is risky for the company; if sales lag and cash flows are not as projected, the business may not be able to meet its short-term credit obligations.

❖ Savings, Friends and Start-ups

The major source of capital for adventure businesses during their start-up is often the personal savings, equipment and credit of the business owners. This is generally a combination of personal cash savings which provide the initial start-up funds, the transfer of personal equipment to the business for operating use, and any short-term personal credit sources such as credit cards or bank lines of credit.

This personal commitment by the owner is often combined with loans, or co-signatures on loans, from friends or relatives in order to expand the capital base available. For the most part, the capital provided by friends and relatives is non-secured by assets.[2]

❖ Trade Credit

Trade credit is where the manufacturer or seller of goods or services extends payment credit for a determined period of time (e.g. 30 days) and allows the purchaser to pay at a later date. Over 40 percent of short-term financing is in the form of accounts payable (trade credit). (*Block, 1994, p. 282*)

❖ Bank Credit

Banks may provide short-term loans or lines of credit to businesses for the financing of operational or seasonal cash flow needs. In this case, the bank will primarily be concerned with the business' ability to generate adequate cash flow to meet the payment demands.

Long-term Financing

Long-term funds generally consist of debt or equity financing that has terms of two years or more. They include the sale of stock, bank loans, the issuance of bonds, and mortgages. To protect against not being able to carry short-term financing during low cash flow periods, companies may rely on long-term financing to purchase fixed assets as well as to finance a portion of current asset (cash) needs. Established companies or companies with collateral tend to have better access to long-term funds than newer companies or those without a significant asset base. This is an issue for many adventure businesses today, and one which restricts the growth of many viable operations (and in fact the entire adventure industry) since they may not have either the stability or the appropriate assets that banks or investors require in order to lend or invest long-term capital.

2 *Secured creditors get priority over shareholders if the business collapses. There are three main types of secured investments: a) General Security Agreement, which gives the investor the right to non-specific assets equal in value to the money advanced as a loan; b) Purchase Money Security Interest, which is tied to a specific asset; and c) Mortgage against property, where the investor has a lien against a building or real estate of the business.*

Table 4-1 ❖ *Marketable Securities and Travel Wholesalers*

*I*n order to better understand the opportunity potential of having good cash flow management, consider the European travel wholesaler who sells 200 individual trips for your adventure company.

Assume:

❖ All trips are sold by European travel agents on behalf of the wholesaler.

❖ You quoted the wholesaler a price of $800 net to you, and it has then marked it up so that the price charged in Europe is $1,000.

❖ The travel agent and wholesaler will each receive 10% of the $1,000 ($100) for each trip sold. You will receive your desired $800.

❖ It costs you $700 in operating costs for each of the 200 people.

❖ The wholesaler has sold the 200 spaces by April 1, and you may invoice the wholesaler in September, once all the trips have been completed.

❖ On April 1, the wholesaler has $200,000 from the sale of your trips and deposits $160,000 in a marketable security which collects 8% interest per annum. The remaining $40,000 (20%) is taken by the agent and wholesaler for their operating costs. This $160,000 will eventually be paid to you.

Between April 1 and October 1 (when you get your money and cash the cheque), the wholesaler makes $6,400 (8% per year X 6 months) on the money it will eventually pay you. After your operating costs, you made $20,000 (200 people X $100 after operating costs). The $6,400 represents an additional 32% income for the wholesaler — over and above the 10% commission originally charged on your product.

❖ **Common Stock**

Common stock (share) represents the ownership interest of the firm. Normally, each share represents one vote in electing the company's board of directors. The board members are responsible to the stockholders, and the stockholders have the authority to elect a new board if desired. As a form of financing, common stock provides the corporation's equity. Corporations sometimes create two classes of common stock, one of which does not have voting rights.

❖ Preferred Stock

Preferred stock is a form of stock which has a fixed dividend (interest similar to a bond) that must be paid before common stock dividends can be paid. It has two important preferences over common stock: preference as to payment of dividends and preference as to stockholders' claims on the assets of the business in the event of bankruptcy. It is an equity security and represents an ownership interest in the company.

❖ Corporate Bond

Bonds are long-term debt agreements issued by corporations (or governments), generally in units of $1,000 principal value per bond. Each bond represents two promises by the issuing organization: the promise to repay the $1,000 principal value at maturity and the promise to pay the stated interest rate (coupon rate) when due. Bonds are seeing increasing use by larger adventure companies as a way to raise capital.[3]

❖ Lease Financing

A long-term, non-cancellable lease is an alternative to the purchase of an asset with borrowed funds. Such lease obligations are a form of long-term financing which must be shown on the balance sheet as debt. Leases are typically used as a form of financing when: a) the business lacks the credit to purchase the asset, but has the cash flow to pay the lease; b) there is no down payment required, which may assist the business' cash flow; c) there may be tax benefits to leasing; and/or d) risk-management considerations determine that it is better not to own the asset.

❖ Mortgages

Mortgages are loan agreements between the business and an investor or bank which require equipment or real estate as collateral for the loan. The issuance of the loan is tied directly to the value of the asset.

Income Statements and Balance Sheets

The two most common financial statements used by financial managers are the income statement and the balance sheet. The income statement provides information on revenues and expenses over a specific period of time, whereas the balance sheet shows the values of assets, liabilities and owners' equity at a specific point in time.

---

3 *As examples of this, within the past few years Belize Point Adventure Resort, Hakai Beach Resort, and the Chic Chocs Wilderness Resort have all attempted bond issues.*

Figure 4-2 ✧ Finance Decision Making

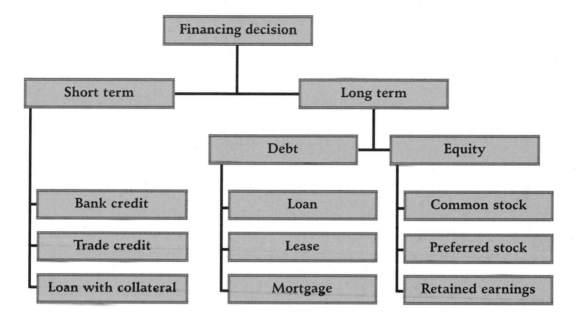

The income statement is the major tool used to measure cash flow and profitability of a business over a period of time. An income statement may be for any length of defined time that analysis is required: the length of a trip, an operating season, a month, a number of months, or a year.

Analysis of income statements for past operating periods allows for critical observation of "how the business has done" over the period — relative to previous expectations or past performance, or compared to other businesses.

The construction of "pro forma" income statements allows for a certain level of forecasting and cost/benefit analysis to be done for a future period. In this manner, a manager may predict future revenues, upcoming expenses and projected profits. Within the adventure industry, pro forma income statements are primarily a compilation of operating costs (budgeted and projected trip costs) along with the fixed costs the company will incur over the period.

The balance sheet shows what the business owns and what obligations it has, along with how assets are financed by liabilities or ownership interest. The balance sheet is intended to show what the business is worth, how financially flexible it is, and how liquid it is.

Since the balance sheet is a representation of the business on a specific date, it does not attempt to show results over a specific period of time. Comparisons of one balance sheet with another for the same business will, however, provide information on changes in position during the time which has passed between the two "snapshots".

Table 4-2 ❖ Pro Forma Income Statements

The Adventure Company, Inc.
Pro Forma Income Statement
for the year ended December 31, 1996

Sales of Okanagan and Baja trips $156,260

Cost of Goods Sold
    Variable Trip Costs
    Okanagan (food and gas) 7,508
    Baja (food and gas) 18,000
    Wages: Guides 27,300
    Promotion 1,000
    Travel 600
Total cost of goods sold $54,408

Gross profit 101,852
Selling and administrative expense 75,694
Operating profit $26,158

Net income before taxes 26,158
Taxes (33%) 8,632
Net income $17,526

A complete business plan for "The Adventure Company" can be found in the Appendix at the end of this text.

The "net worth" of a business (book value) is determined by taking everything the business owns and subtracting the debt obligations. What remains is the stockholders' equity, representing the business' net worth. The "market value" of a business will often vary widely from the net worth value of that business. This is largely due to the business being worth whatever the buyer actually thinks it is worth. Factors may include: industry outlook, growth prospects, risk-return expectations, market position, permit values and entry barriers.

     Although there is no hard-and-fast rule regarding how to value what a business is worth, many financial managers consider the book value plus one year's sales revenue a suitable place to begin the valuation process. In the case above of "The Adventure Company Inc.", this approach would bring the starting valuation to $174,286 ($156,260 sales plus $18,026 book value).

Table 4-3 ❖ Balance Sheet
The Adventure Company, Inc.
Pro Forma Income Statement
as of December 31, 1996

Assets

Current Assets

Cash	33,413
(less income tax)	8,632
equals	24,781
Prepaid expenses (vehicle insurance)	500
Total current assets	**25,281**

Capital Assets

Office equipment / Misc. equipment	4,475
Boats and equipment	40,770
Office supplies	200
Total capital assets	**45,445**

Total assets	**$70,726**

Liabilities and Stockholders' Equity

Liabilities

GST payable	7,688
Accumulated amortization	4,524
Note payable to owner	16,724
Note payable to bank	23,764
Total liabilities	**52,700**

Stockholders' Equity

Retained earnings	17,526
Contributed capital, common shares	500
(50,000 Class "A" shares at $ 0.01 ea.)	
Total stockholders' equity	**18,026**

Total liabilities and stockholders' equity	**$70,726**

Fixed and Variable Costs

The word *cost* can have different meanings depending on the context in which it is used. Costs are classified into either fixed or variable. Fixed costs are those expenses which do not vary with sales: expenses that are incurred whether or not any sales are made. Fixed costs may include such things as: marketing, insurance, administration costs and depreciation.

Variable costs are expenses which vary directly with sales — those costs that are incurred only if sales are made and trips operate — and are often called operating expenses. Variable costs may include such things as: guest food, program expenses, transportation expenses and wages for contracted guides.

Any revenue which remains after the business covers all variable and fixed costs is excess and becomes profit (net income) which the owners may spend as they see fit. If revenues do not cover both variable and fixed costs, the business loses money in that time period. The point where revenue meets both variable and fixed costs exactly is the point where the business breaks even. Table 4-4 shows the types of costs that are categorized as either fixed or variable.

Bottom-up Budgeting

One of the first financial tools that both guides and adventure operators develop is the bottom-up budgeting of a proposed trip. This is, in essence, a short-term pro forma income statement. Bottom-up budgeting entails the construction of a trip budget which calculates, and balances, the trip revenue from participant registration numbers as well as the total costs of operating the trip.[5]

Total revenue is easily calculated by multiplying the number of expected trip participants by the amount charged for the trip. Total costs of the trip include the per-participant costs incurred by running the trip (variable costs), as well as a contribution to the firm's annual fixed costs and profit. ***Break-even for the trip is calculated as the point at which the sales revenue covers:***

❖ *the trip's per-participant operating expenses*

❖ *a suitable portion of the firm's annual fixed expenses*

❖ *a suitable portion of the firm's annual profit expectations*

The amount of sales revenue that remains after operating expenses have been deducted and that can be used to contribute towards the covering of fixed expenses and profit is referred to as the program's contribution margin. The concept of contribution margin is central to the ability to forecast the true break-even point of either a trip or a year's operations.

---

5 *"Top down" budgeting (applicable to a wide variety of applications such as trip budgets, marketing budgets and insurance budgets.) takes place when a business determines it has a specific amount of money for the specific function, and carries out the task for this amount. For example, insurance coverage purchased for $400 — because that is what the company can afford — is a top-down budget. Compare this to a bottom-up budget, based on questions such as: "What are our risks?" "What risks do we insure, and which do we retain?" and "With these questions answered, what will adequate insurance cost us?"*

In order to construct bottom-up income statements for a business (or an individual trip budget), one must be able to accurately calculate both revenue and expense for the period. The key to doing this is to accurately determine the revenue and expense categories that are relevant. These categories are called accounts and form the basis of a business' budget forecasting as well as of the overall accounting system. Table 4-4 shows the types of revenue and expense accounts used for the hypothetical "Western Guiding Inc." Note that the expense accounts fall into either fixed or variable categories.

Ratio Analysis

Financial ratios are used to weigh and evaluate the operating performance of a business. In order for the ratios to mean much to the user, they must be compared with some sort of trend or industry standard, for example, the trend of the past performance of the same business, or ratio norms within the same industry. Because the adventure industry is relatively new and there has been little public information shared between businesses regarding financial ratios, ratio analysis for most operators will be of interest when applied to the trends of their own business, but of limited use when compared with other businesses lacking similar information. As the industry matures, comparative analysis will become easier.

Although there are additional analytical ratios to those presented below, four primary categories containing 13 significant ratios are generally used. Some are more suitable for manufacturing or retail businesses (i.e. asset utilization ratios), while the remainder can be usefully applied to adventure businesses.

A. Profitability Ratios
Profitability ratios measure the efficiency and performance of a business by comparing net income to sales, assets or equity. The *profit margin* reflects the business' cost controls and pricing strategy. The *return on investment* measures the business' use of capital, which in turn reflects how much return on investment creditors and investors will achieve. *Return on equity* measures the return to the business owners, based on book value (net worth). The higher the number, expressed as a percentage, the better the trend.

> *1. Profit margin*
> *2. Return on investment (assets)*
> *3. Return on equity*

B. Liquidity Ratios
Liquidity ratios measure the ability of a business to convert short-term assets to cash (i.e. cash and easily converted securities). High ratios tend to represent inefficient business management. The *current ratio* measures current assets with current liabilities. The *quick ratio* is most suitable for businesses which carry some form of sellable inventory.

> *4. Current ratio*
> *5. Quick ratio*

Table 4-4 ✦ *Sample Revenue and Expense Accounts*

Western Guiding Inc. Income Statement
January 1, 1996 – December 31, 1996

Revenue
General

Canoeing	21,587.88
Hiking	6,615.00
Rafting	10,604.67
Rentals	2,251.95
Helicopter transport	6,400.00
Total general	**$47,459.50**

Sundry

Interest	14.75
Other	3,956.68
Total sundry	**$3,971.43**

Total revenue	**$51,430.93**

Expenses
Fixed Costs

Deprec.: buildings	4,431.07
Deprec.: equipment	5,554.58
Deprec.: vehicle	383.25
Deprec.: net	*10,368.90*
Advertising	5,936.09
Bank charges	222.38
Finance charges	6,345.00
Insurance	4,162.00
Lic./Fees/Dues	195.00
Office	656.57
Postage	873.6
Prof. fees	467.68
Lease	1,088.44
Staff training	0.00
Telephone	1,452.96
Utilities	0.00
Wages (owner)	4,640.73
UIC expense	394.1
CPP expense	235.9
Income tax	1,059.22
Wages: net	6,329.95
WCB	162.24
Total fixed	**$38,260.81**

Variable Costs

Accommodation	213.84
Food	5,570.45
Guide contracts	3,778.00
Helicopter: service	1,001.20
Helicopter: transport	6,771.99
Refunds	1,050.00
Repairs and maintenance	1,214.11
Supplies	2,372.27
Vehicle	3,087.74
Total variable	**$25,059.60**

Total expense	**$63,320.41**
Income	**$–11,889.48**

C. Debt Utilization Ratios

Debt utilization ratios measure the nature of a business' debt management policies. *Debt to total assets* measures the amount of short-term and long-term debt the business has in relation to its total assets; the lower this ratio the better. *Times interest earned* measures how many times the income before interest and taxes covers the interest obligations of the business; the higher this ratio the better. *Fixed charge coverage* measures the business' ability to pay all debts rather than interest alone; the higher this ratio the better.

> 6. *Debt to total assets*
> 7. *Times interest earned*
> 8. *Fixed charge coverage*

D. Asset Utilization Ratios

Asset utilization ratios measure the utilization of business assets. *Receivables turnover* measures the number of times per year receivables turn over relative to sales; generally, the more times receivables turn over, the better, unless a shorter collection period has a negative effect on credit sales. *Average collection period* measures the number of days it takes to collect money owing from clients; generally, the less time it takes to collect receivables the better. *Inventory turnover* measures the number of times the business' inventory turns over each year; generally, the more times inventory turns over, the better, depending on whether or not there is adequate inventory carried. *Fixed asset turnover* measures the amount of fixed assets the business owns relative to sales; the more sales achieved with the least fixed asset amount, the better. *Total asset turnover* measures the amount of total assets relative to sales.

> 9. *Receivables turnover*
> 10. *Average collection period*
> 11. *Inventory turnover*
> 12. *Fixed asset turnover*
> 13. *Total asset turnover*

The examples on the following page are based on the data from The Adventure Company Income Statement and Balance Sheet found in Figures 4-2 and 4-3.

Financial Analysis of Private Companies

Care must be taken when applying ratio analysis to privately owned adventure businesses. In many cases standard financial statements only portray part of the story, due to a number of significant and unique characteristics:

Table 4-5 ✦ A Sample Ratio Analysis

A. Profitability Ratios		The Adventure Company	Industry Average
1. Profit margin =	$\dfrac{\text{Net income}}{\text{Sales}}$	$\dfrac{\$17,526}{\$156,260} = 11.2\%$	2%
2. Return on investment =	$\dfrac{\text{Net income}}{\text{Total assets}}$	$\dfrac{\$17,526}{\$70,726} = 25\%$	13%
3. Return on equity =	$\dfrac{\text{Net income}}{\text{Stockholder equity }^a}$	$\dfrac{\$17,526}{\$18,026} = 97\%$	75%

B. Liquidity Ratios

4. Current ratio =	$\dfrac{\text{Current assets}}{\text{Current liabilities}}$	$\dfrac{\$25,281}{\$12,212} = 2.07$	1.0%
5. Quick ratio =	$\dfrac{\text{Current assets (Inventory)}}{\text{Current liabilities}}$	n/a	n/a

C. Debt Utilization Ratios

6. Debt to total assets =	$\dfrac{\text{Total debt}}{\text{Total assets}}$	$\dfrac{\$52,700}{\$70,726} = 75\%$	125%
7. Times interest earned =	$\dfrac{\text{Income before I \& T}^b}{\text{Interest}}$	n/a	n/a
8. Fixed charge coverage =	$\dfrac{\text{Income BFC \& T}^c}{\text{Fixed charges}}$	n/a	n/a

D. Asset Utilization Ratios

9. Receivables turnover =	$\dfrac{\text{Sales}}{\text{Receivables}}$	n/a	n/a
10. Average collection period =	$\dfrac{\text{Accounts receivable}}{\text{Average daily credit sales}}$	n/a	n/a
11. Inventory turnover =	$\dfrac{\text{Cost of goods sold}}{\text{Inventory}}$	n/a	n/a
12. Fixed asset turnover =	$\dfrac{\text{Sales}}{\text{Fixed assets}}$	$\dfrac{\$156,260}{\$45,445} = 3.4\%$	17.0%
13. Total asset turnover =	$\dfrac{\text{Sales}}{\text{Total assets}}$	$\dfrac{\$156,260}{\$70,726} = 2.2\%$	7.4%

a. *Stockholder equity here is $500 common stock and $17,562 retained earnings*
b. *I&T = Interest and Taxes*
c. *BFC&T = Before Fixed Charges and Taxes*

❖ Debt and Equity

The level of debt carried by an adventure business is likely to be related to the extent to which its owners will assume personal financial risk. Owners are likely to access more debt only by agreeing to personally back the loans if the business is unable to repay them. Due to this fact, they may be willing to restrict business growth and depress profits in order to eliminate some of this personal financial risk. Many adventure business owners are more comfortable with the physical risk associated with their adventure sports than with the financial risks associated with owning a risky and uncertain business.

❖ Lifestyle Considerations

Lifestyle considerations have a tendency to affect balance sheet numbers. In some cases assets are inflated by real estate or equipment which is for personal use by the owners. In others the balance sheet will fail to show assets the owner owns separately but uses (possibly in a crucial way) for the operation of the business. Return on investment and return on equity may be distorted when the owners hold assets outside of the business. Before return on investment or equity calculations are completed, it may be necessary to include the assets or equity that are part of the business, whether or not the business or owner holds them.

Income statements may be distorted due to spending on items such as owner recreation or transportation which artificially inflate expenses. This is often done so that the owner may benefit from the spending, while minimizing impact from taxes.

Many adventure operators have lifestyle-related motivations for owning their own business and they are less concerned with making the business grow than with creating and maintaining a desirable outdoor- and travel-oriented lifestyle. This often masks the potential growth opportunities of their business and may make both the income statement and balance sheet appear weaker than their potential.

❖ Risk Management

It has become common practice for adventure companies to hold assets in a second company separate from the primary, operating company for purposes of risk management in the event of a lawsuit. These assets are then leased to the primary company on the assumption that any lawsuit brought against the business would need to be brought against the primary company and that the assets would be protected in the second, separate company. In this case balance sheets will not accurately show the fixed assets required to operate the business, but will only show the current assets and receivables from sales.

❖ Short-term Capital

Financial theory suggests that the use of capital be balanced between short- and long-term sources. Small-business owners, who do not normally have ready access to long-term capital, will tend to finance fixed assets any way they can, and this may impact on the type of debt that shows on the balance sheet.

References

Block, S., et al. ***Foundations of Financial Management***. Irwin Inc., 1994.

Garrison, R., et al. ***Managerial Accounting***. 3rd Canadian ed. Irwin Inc., 1996.

Hilton, R. ***Managerial Accounting***. McGraw-Hill Inc., 1991.

Meigs, R., et al. ***Financial Accounting***. McGraw-Hill Ryerson Ltd., 1991.

Chapter Five

Stages of Business Growth

Small businesses pass through identifiable "life cycle" or development stages as they grow and develop. Different businesses do not develop at the same speed, and many may stay in one stage for considerable periods of time. This may be due to either the nature of the activity or the personal desires and ambitions of the owners. The transition from one "stage" to another often brings with it new and unique issues to deal with; crises may develop as the business requires new levels of expertise in order to thrive. Business owners need to be able to identify where their business is on its development curve and what additional management skills and resources are required to assist in the transition from one stage to another.

Inception and Incubation

The first step in incubating a business is the development of an idea and a vision. The main priorities of the business will be those of its originator, and his or her perspective and "world view" will dictate the business' initial direction. Primary efforts will revolve around creating a commercially viable product and testing it within the marketplace. Emphasis will be upon creating a positive cash flow, developing sellable products, and managing and administering business activities. Start-up financing sources may be owner savings and personal short-term credit.

❖ Market- or Product-driven Inception

As a theoretical marketing rule, business developers are advised to develop products which are market- (i.e. client-) driven, which means that market demands dictate interest and viability in a certain product. Within the adventure industry, however, where operators tend to be "lifestyle adventurers" who have specific personal skill and experience sets to act as the incubators for new products, there has been much grieving by unsuccessful business owners who could not understand why they could not sell products which both revolved around their specific expertise and would let them develop a specific lifestyle. This product-driven approach has gradually given way to the economic realities of a more educated and demanding market.

Development and Survival

Once a business reaches this stage, it likely has potential to survive. It now needs to develop both its organization and its product levels. As the business grows, there will be a need to access financing in order to expand its operations and to finance the purchase of fixed assets. The owners will need to manage increasing operational demands. Bank lines of credit or short-term loans are common.

Many adventure businesses stay in this stage for an extended length of time. Service quality may be affected if growth outpaces equipment inventories or staffing resources.

Figure 5-1✧ Business Development Stages

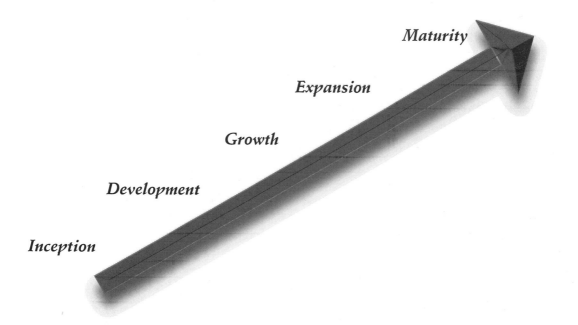

Maturity

Expansion

Growth

Development

Inception

As the need for sales growth increases, so does the necessity to expand the customer base. This means diversifying, offering new products, increasing marketing channels and possibly operating in new geographic locations. Such expansion affects the amount of control the owners can have over operational matters and may bring new types of customers.

If the business is successful, competitors will attempt to enter the market and entry barriers will begin to play an important role in profitability. Accounting and cost controls will become important to the efficiency of the business.

In some cases the owners may be able to sell the business at this point to purchasers who can envision the business' potential and who have the financial wherewithal and management ability to "grow the company". In others, the business may fail completely even though it shows significant cash flow. This is often the result of its inability to access the long-term financing from investors or banks that is necessary for expansion.

Growth

In many ways this stage typifies the entire adventure industry in the 1990s. Through the 1980s many adventure products were both developed and proved viable; the 1990s have provided significant growth both for the industry as a whole and for businesses which hold market position.

By the time a business reaches this stage, it is likely to be profitable but may not be generating much equity for the owners since earnings may need to be retained and invested back into the business to finance further growth.

The business may require expansion into new markets and/or new geographic locations in order to maintain growth. Owners may require the further development of administrative and management knowledge and competence. The supervision of staff will play a prominent role for managers. External financing and access to long-term capital will become important in complementing higher cash flows and in financing required fixed assets.

In most cases the owners are able to sell the business at this point for a significant profit. Issues which have arisen during recent attempts to sell this size of adventure business include the following: businesses at this stage still require hands-on involvement of the owners in operational matters; there are a limited number of individuals with both this type of expertise and access to the funds to purchase this stage of business; and those who do have access to this level of financing may not feel comfortable with the financial risk associated with such a purchase. These factors create exit barriers to owners who want out of their business but find it too large to sell to another person with similar skills and interests.

When owners of adventure businesses find they are unable to sell their business, it often has the result of making the business worth more "alive" than "dead".[1] That is, the owner ends up operating the business in order to take out money on an annual basis from operations rather than from the sale of the business.

Amalgamations, consolidations and joint ventures are beginning to characterize this development stage within the adventure industry as ways for companies to become more cost-effective and to enable them to access new, further-afield trip offerings.

Expansion and Maturity

The expansion of a business is its period of maturation and includes activities such as acquisitions, franchising and large market-growth drives for reasons of market power or defense. In reality, there are very few adventure businesses which have achieved this level. Most adventure operators and resorts are too new in their life cycle to have gone through the growth stage. The closest examples of this stage within the industry are likely companies such as Mountain Travel*Sobek and Canadian Mountain Holidays, representing a very small number of very large adventure companies.

Cost controls, professional management, administrative paperwork, formal accounting systems, organizational systems and dividend payouts are characteristic of firms in this stage. Large amounts of long-term financing are required. "Professional" management which does not have the same lifestyle commitment to the business will have been introduced.

[1] *Thanks to Neil Hartling for these terms.*

References

Kao, R. ***Entrepreneurship and Enterprise Development***. Holt, Rinehart and Winston of Canada Ltd., 1989.

Long, W., and W. McMullan. ***Developing New Ventures***. Harcourt Brace Jovanovich Inc., 1990.

Maurice, C., et al. ***Managerial Economics***. Irwin Inc., 1992.

O'Hara, P. ***The Total Business Plan***. John Wiley and Sons Inc., 1990.

Steinmetz, L. ***Critical Stages of Small Business Growth***. Business Horizons, 1969.

Chapter Six

Business Plan Development

A business plan is a document which articulates the critical aspects, basic assumptions and financial projections regarding a business venture. It is also a basic document used to attract interest and support — financial and otherwise — for a new business concept. It is generally used as a means of attracting capital and guiding growth. The process of writing a business plan is an invaluable experience, for it forces the entrepreneur to think through his or her business concept in a systematic way. This chapter is intended to outline one format for a business plan and to discuss the issues encountered by most entrepreneurs as they prepare their plan.

One of the reasons a good plan is so difficult to write is that it has a multitude of purposes. The plan is a blueprint for the company itself, and as such is intended to help the firm's management. The plan is also typically used to attract potential investors. Finally, the plan may serve as the legal document with which funds are raised. Thus, it becomes extremely critical to understand exactly what purpose the plan is serving, and for which audience it is intended. The first rule is to keep in mind who the reader is and to make sure the document addresses his or her particular concerns.

This may mean that the original business plan will go through a number of versions as it is reused for a number of different purposes: as a feasibility study, for attracting investors, for the articulation of partnership relations, for bank loan applications and for the ongoing evaluation of how the business is evolving in relation to its original goals, objectives and timelines. A business plan is a document that may serve many purposes. In order for it to be effective, it must be well-written and professionally edited, printed and bound prior to its circulation. *For a complete example of a business plan, see Appendix A.*

General Requirements of the Plan

It is important that the plan be relatively short (20 to 40 pages) and clearly written. Write the document with the reader in mind: is he or she an investor, a banker, a potential partner? Do not assume the reader will be an expert in the service or market the business is concerned with. Think of the plan as an argument: every point made offers an opportunity to support the business' claims.

The Executive Summary

These few pages (two to four) form the most critical piece of any business plan. Investors will turn immediately to this section in order to get their first impression of the venture. To ensure that this section encompasses all that it should, it is best written last. The executive summary should be able to act as a stand-alone abstract which gives a brief overview of the entire plan.

The executive summary must clearly but briefly explain:

> ❖ *The company's status and its management*
>
> ❖ *The company's products or services, and the benefits they provide to users*
>
> ❖ *The market and competition for the service*
>
> ❖ *A summary of the company's financial prospects*
>
> ❖ *The amount of money needed, and how it will be used*

The Company

This section should describe the company's origins, objectives and management. It should indicate how the company will be organized, who will fill the various roles and what their responsibilities will be. Some background on the founders should be given, and their more extensive resumes referenced in an attachment or appendix section. The "story" of how the business came into being should be briefly told so that potential investors get some sense of the company's history. The section should describe the current status of the company: number of employees, sales and profits (if any), products, services, facilities, etc. Finally, this section should paint a picture of where the company hopes to go and how it envisions getting there, i.e. its strategy.

The Product or Service

Having introduced the product in the previous section, the plan should describe it in more detail here. What needs does the product meet, especially compared to competing products? Discussions on product positioning are especially useful here. If the product exists and is in use, detailed descriptions of its usage and the results, plus some customer testimonials, will prove valuable. If the product has yet to be put together, an explanation of what is intended and of the key milestones in the process is important.

The Market

A common mistake is to deal with the market portion of the plan in a cursory manner or to make the business plan a marketing plan. Although the document is not intended to be the company marketing plan, investors want evidence that the founders of the company have studied the market, understand it and are driven by their desire to satisfy its needs. To convey this, the plan should address:

❖ ***The size, rate of growth, and purchasing characteristics of the target market***

Investors will be interested in — and will want to make sure the entrepreneurs are interested in and understand — market segments, the buying process and how purchase decisions are made.

❖ ***The company's perspective on the market***

Investors will be curious about the entrepreneurs' perspective on the market. Why does the company think it is bringing something new to the market? What trends in the market does the company see, and what specific changes does the company anticipate in the future?

❖ ***The reaction the company expects from the market***

What hurdles does the company expect in introducing its product? How will it overcome them? What features and benefits does the company expect will be particularly popular?

If there is a marketing plan for the company, this information should come almost directly from that document. If there is not, this information will form an outline for its development.

Competition

No business plan is complete without a section which describes the competing firms and products. Investors want to be assured that the entrepreneurs are aware of (and understand) their potential competitors. Information on competitors' products, prices and marketing approaches should be included.

Sales and Marketing

This section of the plan should explain the manner in which the product will reach its customers. The plan should describe how target customers will be identified and how awareness will be built through advertising, promotion or direct mail. The plan should also detail how the product will be sold. This section should also address how the company will introduce its product to the marketplace. This might include public relations, advertisement, special promotions or targeted growth.

Operations

In this section, explain how the product will be packaged, what facilities will be required, where operations will occur, how employees or contractors will be used, what equipment will be required, etc.

Financial

In this section, investors expect to see realistic financial projections, typically for a three- to five-year horizon. The following information should be included: an income statement, balance sheet, cash flow forecast and break-even analysis.

It is critical that the financials be driven by thoroughly documented assumptions. For instance, do not just develop a sales forecast. Present detailed assumptions about package price and sales volume. The same is true for expenses.

While it is impossible to know what is going to happen in the future, investors will familiarize themselves with other firms in the industry in order to develop a sense of the appropriateness of the numbers and forecast. Once they are satisfied that the projections are realistic, they will use these same financials to help them value the firm and calculate a potential price for their investment. Someone who is part of the management team must have the ability to develop income statement and cash flow forecasts and budgets.

This section should also clearly state the amount of money being sought, and how it will be used.

Attachments

The resumes of all key personnel and an explanation of their responsibilities should be included in this section. In addition, any sample product literature, letters from customers or suppliers, etc. can be included.

References

Kao, R. ***Entrepreneurship and Enterprise Development***. Holt, Rinehart and Winston of Canada Ltd., 1989.

Long, W. ,and W. McMullan. ***Developing New Ventures***. Harcourt Brace Jovanovich Inc., 1990.

Massarella, G., et al. ***How to Prepare a Business Plan***. American Management Association, 1993.

O'Hara, P. ***The Total Business Plan***. John Wiley and Sons Inc., 1990.

Touchie, R. ***Preparing a Successful Business Plan***. 2nd ed. International Self Council Press Inc. 1993.

Chapter Seven

Start-up Action Plans

Being confident that there is an adequate market demand for a business and having worked through the business planning stages creates a reasonable basis from which to begin planning the business start-up and its implementation. The business founder must determine what resources are required and in what order they will be needed to launch a new venture. Many aspiring business founders tend to underestimate the resources needed to get the business to the stage where it can be self-supporting, and as a result will underfinance their needs.

In addition to financial and human resource needs, there are many philosophical and legal considerations regarding the business that must be worked out with other founders and investors. Likely the most common cause of future grief within a business is the disparate goals and expectations of the different players within the business, whether they be business partners, investors or employees.

The following section is intended to provide a non-definitive list of business start-up considerations that need to be articulated prior to the business becoming operational — particularly between prospective partners. A clear, concise and realistic working-through of the following subjects prior to the investment of funds on the part of partners and investors will help to alleviate future differing viewpoints which could ultimately prove detrimental to the business' health.[1]

Mission Statement

A mission statement is the unique purpose that sets a business apart from other businesses of its type. A mission statement reflects a firm's strengths and specific competencies. It identifies the contribution the firm intends to make in terms of its products offered and the markets it intends to serve, and is important as a method for founders, investors and employees to be clear as to what the business is about.

Often a mission statement will reflect a company's philosophy, values, aspirations, priorities and desired public image. It is not changed frequently but is sometimes modified as a result of changes in a company's opportunities, strengths, risks and weaknesses.

Personal Strengths and Weaknesses

Aspiring entrepreneurs frequently make haphazard judgments about the staffing resources required to run a business. Friends and relatives are invited to participate, more out of a sense of obligation than because of an identified expertise the business may need. Similarly, business partners may choose to adopt a specific role within the business more by default than because of expertise.

[1] *This chapter is largely based on material provided by Greg Foweraker.*

Businesses need to be very careful at the start-up stages about how they select individuals to fill required roles, and partners need to converse openly about their personal strengths, weaknesses and interests in order to fill appropriate functions within the business. It is especially important to ensure that there is no overlapping of roles and that job descriptions are developed for each individual.

Investment Risk and Return

There are many different places where individuals can invest their money instead of in an adventure business. Other options may have more security of capital, greater or lesser financial rewards, or more liquidity, etc., and the importance of each element will vary with each individual. It is important for business partners and investors to be clear about, and agree on, the amount of risk there is to invested capital, the likely rate of returns, the timelines the returns are based on, etc.

Lifestyle Goals

The likelihood of a number of business partners having exactly the same lifestyle and financial goals in any business is slim. However, because adventure businesses are so closely related to the previous recreational pursuits and lifestyle aspirations of their founders, there is a high chance that the business philosophy of "lifestylers" who want to get into a business to support their personal lifestyle interests will vary greatly from that of the investment-focused partner who sees an opportunity to make substantial money but is less interested in whether he or she is selling travel trips to Central America or widgets in Toronto. In such a situation, business operations may get caught between the partners' greatly differing philosophical approaches.

Capital Sources and Types of Investment

As adventure sport activities gain acceptance within society, the industry is seeing broader sources of investment capital. Whereas in the past, sources of investment were limited largely to personal contacts, family and friends, today the industry is able to access funds through venture capital, bank loans, lines of credit, bonds, mortgages, time-share arrangements and stock sales. This leaves the business partners with a wide variety of both equity- and debt-financing sources; however, individuals vary greatly in their comfort level with different sources of investment.

Whether or not the business will sell ownership shares in the company, and how much ownership partners are prepared to give away, needs to be decided upon. So, too, does their tolerance for debt financing in the way of bank loans, bonds and investor loans.

Pricing Strategy

It is important for business partners to decide prior to business start-up on their product's positioning in terms of quality and price. A business which has one partner who envisions a top-quality, high-end product while the other is targeting an economy client is in for either disappointed clients or potentially low sales.

Credit

From automobiles to houses and from dinners to travel trips, people buy on credit every day. An adventure business becomes a creditor when it sells a trip to a client and allows the client to pay in some form other than cash. This may be done by allowing a deposit upon booking and then collecting the remainder of the fee at a later date, by allowing the client to pay in instalments or by allowing payment via credit card.

Any decision to allow a client to purchase a trip on credit is a marketing decision, a cash flow decision and a philosophical decision. It is a marketing decision because it has the effect of making it easier for the client to purchase the trip. It is a cash flow decision because it impacts the business' current and future cash flows according to the terms of the credit and when the monies will be collected. It is a philosophical decision since it determines how the business will allow clients to pay for their trip and whether or not the business will play a part in providing them with a source of short-term financing.

Corporate Structure

Individual roles, staffing needs, the need for job descriptions, the chain of command, administrative responsibilities, field operation responsibilities, risk management, financial controls, purchasing methods, financial signing authority and other related topics all need to be decided upon prior to the start-up of the business.

Corporate Values and Ethics

Environmental impact philosophy for trips, helicopter use and noise impacts, rescue and evacuation of injured clients, company definitions of terminology such as "eco-tourism", financial contribution to local economies while operating in the Third World, business ethics, the value placed upon risk management, and related ethics all need to be considered prior to the start-up of the business.

Management Considerations

In order for the founding partners to be fairly compensated for their sweat equity during the start-up stages of the business, an equitable reimbursement for their expertise, time and energy needs to be determined. This contribution is seldom equal during the start-up stages; reimbursement should be discussed early, rather than leaving it until later.

In addition, the possibility of a partner leaving the business needs to be considered. What kind of buy-out clause should the business have for the partners? Can a partner sell his or her ownership shares without other partners having a right of first refusal? Should the business be required to carry director death insurance so that it can afford to purchase that partner's ownership shares?

Business Risk

The amount of tolerance for risk to the business will also vary between partners. This is primarily an issue of the level of risk each partner is comfortable with for the business, and the specific risk management techniques the business should implement. Should the business operate without liability insurance? Should the business carry rescue and evacuation insurance for clients? Should the business hire its guides as employees or use contract-for-service guides? What guide qualifications should the business require? Should the business have all clients sign waivers? Should the business use indemnification forms for parents of minors? These are all questions which need to be answered prior to starting business operations.

References

Daft, R., and P. Fitzgerald. *Management*. 1st Canadian ed. Holt, Rinehart and Winston of Canada Ltd., 1992.

Dubrin, A,. and D. Ireland. *Management and Organization*. 2nd ed. South-Western Publishing Co., 1993.

Long, W,. and W. McMullan. *Developing New Ventures*. Harcourt Brace Jovanovich Inc., 1990.

Pearce, J., and R. Robinson. *Formulation, Implementation, and Control of Competitive Strategy*. Richard D. Irwin, 1991.

Chapter Eight

Adventure Product Development

As discussed in Chapter One, today many adventure businesses develop, market and provide services within the tourism industry. Tourists as clientele bring with them a very different set of expectations and demands. The adventure activity is no longer being sought after by the client solely as a way to become proficient in an activity, or to increase his or her perception of self, but for holiday and actualization purposes. For the business owner, this requires a whole new range of skill sets in order to both tap into the tourist as a client and provide the service levels he or she expects. This chapter discusses various selected topics of interest which pertain specifically to the development and marketing of adventure tourism activities.

Characteristics of Tourism

Tourism carries its own defining set of characteristics, of which product developers need to be aware. Some of these are:

❖ *As in other service industries, tourism products are produced by the business and consumed by the guest at the same time.*

❖ *Supply cannot be stored ahead of time to be distributed slowly at some time in the future, and capacity must be determined ahead of time by the operator.*

❖ *Often the tourism product cannot be inspected ahead of time by the purchaser, since intangible experiences and memories are being sold.*

❖ *Products are perceived by guests in terms of "benefits", and packaging trips is the art of bundling these benefits.*

❖ *Travellers purchase products which are consistent with their personal self-image; they will tend to neither purchase above or below this perception.*

❖ *External considerations such as culture, leisure time available, stage of life, age, income, sex and education will all impact the purchasing characteristics of the tourist.*

❖ *Income spent on travel is discretionary spending and is spent at the expense of something else.*

Positioning Adventure Products

The increasing number of adventure products entering the marketplace dictates the need for businesses to find specific niches in order to fill their trips and become profitable. The lack of substantial entry barriers in the industry to date (such as exclusive permits or high levels of capital investment) has enabled businesses to easily enter the marketplace. Thus greater efforts are required on the part of programmers in order to create identifiable differences between themselves and their competitors and to clearly communicate the position of their product to customers.

Product positioning is the consumer's mental perception of the product, which may or may not differ from the actual characteristics of a product. Positioning is usually carried out by a combination of: product type, product price, services provided, promotion techniques, distribution channels and packaging.

Good product positioning is achieved by means of differentiating the product in the mind of the consumer, communicating the benefits of the product to the customer and attempting to strengthen the image by providing information which leads the customer to have certain expectations that can be satisfied by the product. These elements, when combined, help communicate what the product is to the targeted market.

Product Positioning Maps

Product positioning maps show how consumers perceive products in a market and can be helpful when competitive products are similar. The results are plotted on graphs to help show where the products are positioned in relation to each other and to compare two features of the products. They can be used to compare features of competitor products (e.g. what level of service quality is provided for what price), or to compare different features of a company's own products (e.g. how effective a product is in achieving the company's goals versus how much profit it makes for the company).

Positioning maps are also useful when attempting to identify product opportunities since they can show areas that are not being serviced by the marketplace.

Figure 8-1 shows one perception of the backcountry-ski product types offered in western Canada by comparing the two features of product quality and product price. Product #1 represents the non-profit-group-owned, ski-in, non-catered backcountry huts; product #2 represents the general heli-ski company position; product #3 represents the newly built, large and comfortable, helicopter-accessed, catered ski-tour lodge; and product #4 represents the older, smaller and less comfortable ski- or helicopter-accessed cabin. It should be obvious that similar comparative analyses may be carried out within each of the backcountry-ski sectors. For example, not all heli-ski companies offer the same price or service even though they may initially appear to provide products to the same market.

Figure 8-2 is a product positioning map which illustrates the popularity of a company's various products (via the number of clients per trip) and the profitability of each type of trip (via the profit amount per client-day on each trip). The "contribution" is the amount of revenue less the direct client costs (on a daily basis), while the "capacity utilization" is the actual

Figure 8-1 ❖ Backcountry-ski Product Positioning Map

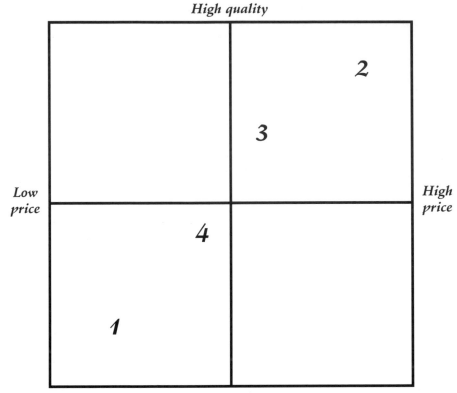

number of clients per trip divided by the capacity of the trip.

The idea of this map is to demonstrate that the company may need to raise or lower prices on selected products to make more money, and/or may need to shift the availability of the products to a more profitable mix. For example, if the products are placed in four cells, as in Figure 8-2, each cell suggests a different pricing tactic to maximize its contribution to the company. For example:

❖ *Offer more products*: For products which make lots of money and fill with clients (the upper left cell), the company could increase the number of trips offered. Adding more Gulf Islands Sea Kayaking and Team Building products would make the company substantially more money.

❖ *Lower prices or increase marketing*: For products which make lots of money but do not fill with clients (upper right cell), the company could lower the trip prices or increase the marketing

Figure 8-2 ❖ Contribution/Capacity Product Positioning Map

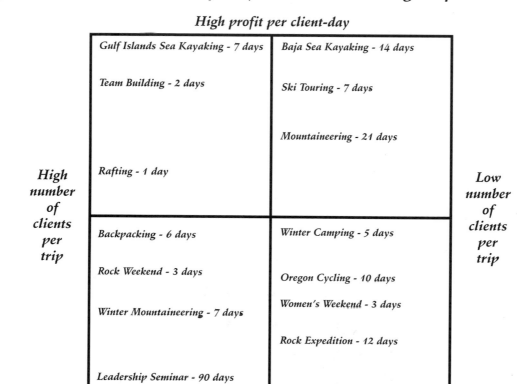

High profit per client-day

Gulf Islands Sea Kayaking - 7 days	*Baja Sea Kayaking - 14 days*
Team Building - 2 days	*Ski Touring - 7 days*
	Mountaineering - 21 days
Rafting - 1 day	

High number of clients per trip ... *Low number of clients per trip*

Backpacking - 6 days	*Winter Camping - 5 days*
Rock Weekend - 3 days	*Oregon Cycling - 10 days*
	Women's Weekend - 3 days
Winter Mountaineering - 7 days	
	Rock Expedition - 12 days
Leadership Seminar - 90 days	

Low profit per client-day

associated with these trips. Increasing the marketing or reducing the prices on the Baja Sea Kayaking or the Ski Touring products would help to fill them; the fact that they are highly profitable leads one to believe there is room to reduce prices and still make a profit.

❖ *Raise prices*: For products which fill with clients but do not make much money (the lower left cell), the company could raise the price of the trips to make them profitable. The Backpacking and Rock Weekend products are examples of this; the fact that they are filled to capacity leads one to believe there is room to raise the prices and still fill the trips.

❖ *Offer fewer courses*: For products which do not fill with clients and do not make money anyway (the lower right cell), the company could decrease the number of offerings and shift these clients to more profitable products. Customers in the Women's Weekend and Rock Expedition products might be encouraged to register in others.

Distribution Channels for Adventure Products

In order for the adventure operator to make a sale to a prospective customer, the product needs to be packaged in a way which will appeal to the customer. In addition, the product needs to be made available to the customer so he or she can purchase it when and if it is decided to do so. The tourism industry has well-defined and unique distribution channels to assist this process. Since the tourism product cannot be stored and is perishable — i.e. a sale lost now cannot be sold later — it is crucial for the operators to get their product into the hands of the right consumer.

❖ *Direct Distribution Channels*

Direct distribution channels are those methods used by the adventure operator to sell his or her package(s) directly to the customer. These methods might include: brochures placed in racks, magazine advertisements, radio advertisements, booth displays, posters, roadside signs and drive-by bookings.

❖ *Indirect Distribution Channels*

Indirect distribution channels are those techniques used when a sale is made through one or more travel trade intermediaries. These intermediaries include:

> ❖ *Tour Wholesalers*: A tour wholesaler is a business which packages any combination of the services of the adventure operator, plus ground transportation, air transportation or accommodation, and sells the resulting package to the customer through some form of sales channel. The packages are usually placed in a catalogue under the wholesaler's name; the adventure company's name seldom appears in the catalogue even though it may be providing the product.
>
> The tour wholesaler does not sell directly to the public but through retail sales outlets such as travel agents. Increasingly, however, wholesalers are selling through their own retail outlets. Wholesalers are compensated through commissions (usually in the 20–30% range) built into the overall package price.
>
> ❖ *Retail Travel Agents*: Travel agents handle the sale and reservation of tours, accommodation, airfares, car rentals, etc. to the consumer, and are paid through commissions from the suppliers. In the case of the travel agent selling a trip packaged by a wholesaler, the travel agent would keep a percentage of the total package price (usually in the 10% range) as his or her commission.
>
> ❖ *Other Intermediaries*: A third indirect channel of distribution used by adventure operators is that of specialty businesses. These might include meeting and convention planners, incentive (reward) travel firms and other specialty sales agencies.

Figure 8-3 ❖ Channels of Distribution

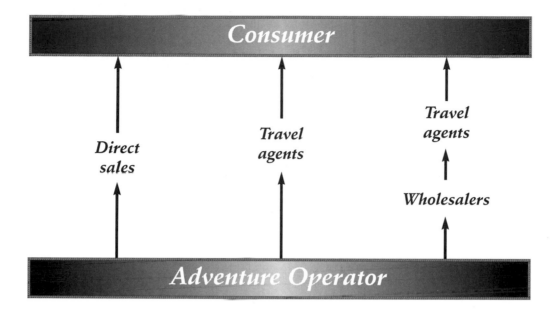

Figure 8-3 shows how the adventure operator can use a variety of different distribution channels to sell the same product to consumers. Historically, most adventure operators have relied upon direct-marketing methods such as brochures, direct mail or media advertising to sell their trips. These methods are adequate for local and regional markets; however, it is usually necessary to use wholesalers as intermediaries to access long-haul, international markets. In fact, one of the indications of a mature adventure tourism business is its ability to convince wholesalers to handle its product(s) in markets that are further afield.

Operator Restrictions and Wholesale Markets

One of the constraints holding wholesalers back from handling a specific adventure operator's products is that of operator stability. Until relatively recently most adventure businesses were small, owner-operated, undercapitalized operations. Many businesses have started up, operated unprofitable trips for a few years, and then their owners have moved on to other ventures. The fact that the wholesaler requires a lead time of two years or more in order to place the operator's trips in its catalogue and market the package, makes the wholesaler very cautious as to whose product it will sell. If there is the chance that the operator will not be in business by the time the wholesaler has sold his or her product, there is little point in attempting to sell the trips. As a result, wholesalers want to see a track record which offers them some stability and comfort level.

In addition, many adventure business owners do not have access to the capital required to expand enough in order to handle the increase in their business resulting from the higher potential volume of wholesaler sales. Although expansion is a good problem for a business to have, wholesalers have the ability to sell an enormous amount of product (relative to what most operators can sell on their own). It must be clear to them that the adventure business has either enough current space to handle the volume, or the financial means to expand its operation appropriately, while not negatively impacting the level of service required.

Another restriction facing wholesalers is whether or not they can sell significant volume of a specific product. Remembering that the wholesaler may only gross 10% of the end price of the package (i.e. $80 of an $800 trip) they must be able to sell large volumes of a product before they are interested in handling it. Some wholesalers express a desire to sell a minimum of $300,000–$500,000 for each page of their product catalogue and attempt to provide catalogue space only for products that can achieve this level of sales. They may do this by providing a complete page for those products that will achieve this, or by providing partial pages for products that will not. It is important for the operator to remember that every $500,000 of sales will gross the wholesaler only 10% of this amount.

Pricing Adventure Products

There are numerous ways for an adventure business to price its products. Price is influenced by such things as product level, competition, company philosophy, market share desired, market expectations and market need. Price must be perceived by the market to be equal to the value received from the experience and is ultimately determined by supply and demand: when supply exceeds demand, the price drops.

The best price for a product is the price that maximizes the difference between total revenue and total costs. Adventure packages tend to be price-elastic, i.e. if the price of a product changes, the volume of sales will also change accordingly.

In pricing, the premise is that the price charged must be sufficient to cover all the costs of trip packaging, administration, marketing and trip operations, plus provide a reasonable profit for the owners. The price charged must cover all variable (operating) costs while also making a contribution to the fixed (overhead) costs. Variable costs are those which are incurred when operating a specific trip. This includes food, supplies, transportation, and guide wages if paid by the guiding day. Fixed costs are those that the business will incur over the year just to be open for business. This includes office expenses, marketing, owner wages and telephone.

The most common approach to the pricing of products is to use some form of "cost plus" pricing. This is done by calculating the "cost base" and then adding some predetermined markup to get the total selling price.

Contribution Approach to Pricing

The contribution approach to pricing consists of calculating the variable expenses associated with providing a product (called the cost base), and adding a suitable markup which will contribute to the fixed costs and profit of the business. The most crucial element of this method is the markup percentage added to the cost base, since it provides the revenue to cover fixed costs and whatever profit (return on investment) is desired.

Table 8-1 shows an example of pricing calculations for a hypothetical business. In this example, the variable costs are defined as those costs that the business will incur per client per trip. The total variable costs per client are calculated to be $300, and a markup of 100% ($300) is added to get the total sale price of the trip. The markup of $300 is the portion that is paid by each client towards covering the annual fixed costs and profit of the business. This is known as the contribution margin, i.e. the amount remaining from sales revenue after variable expenses have been deducted (on a per-person basis). Each package sold provides a certain amount of contribution margin which goes towards covering the business' fixed costs and profit. Generally, the way to increase profits is to increase the contribution margin amount. This can be done by either increasing the markup or decreasing the variable costs.

Table 8-1 ✦ Contribution Approach to Pricing

Variable Costs

Guide wages	80
Trip costs per person	180
Transportation	40
Total variable expenses	**$300**
Markup to cover fixed expenses and profit (100%)	**$300**
Total selling price	**$600**

Break-even Analysis

The break-even point is the point where total sales revenue equals total variable and fixed expenses. Alternatively, it is also the point where the total contribution margin equals the total fixed expenses.

If each package sold contributes something towards the fixed costs, the easiest way to determine how many packages need to be sold in order to break even is to divide the total fixed costs by the contribution margin generated by each client.

$$\frac{\text{Fixed costs}}{\text{Contribution margin per person}} = \text{Break-even point}$$

Consider the example of the Whiteshield Canoe Institute found in Table 8-2. Total fixed costs per year are $35,000. The contribution margin per client is $100 ($250 trip sale price minus $150 variable cost per person). Using the above formula, we can determine that to cover its annual fixed costs the business would have to sell 350 packages.

$$\frac{\$35,000 \text{ fixed costs}}{\$100 \text{ contribution}} = 350 \text{ packages}$$

Table 8-2 ❖ Break-even Point for the Whiteshield Canoe Institute

Weekend Canoe Trip sale price *$250*
Variable expenses per person per trip *$150*
Total fixed costs per year *$35,000*

A similar calculation may be done for the Waddington Ski Tour Company found in Table 8-3. Total fixed costs per year are $60,000. The contribution margin per client is $450 ($700 trip sale price minus $250 variable cost per person). To break even (to cover its annual fixed costs), the business would have to sell 134 packages.

$$\frac{\$60,000 \text{ fixed costs}}{\$450 \text{ contribution}} = 133.3 \text{ packages}$$

Table 8-3 ❖ Break-even Point for the Waddington Ski Tour Company

Ski Trip sale price *$700*
Operating expenses per person per trip *$250*
Total fixed costs per year *$60,000*

After the business sells the required number of packages in order to break even, every package sold beyond this number will contribute a profit amount equal to the contribution margin. For example, for the Waddington Ski Tour Company above, every additional customer above 134 makes the company $450. Since the revenue from the first 134 customers covers all of the company's annual fixed costs, the contribution margin from each additional customer is profit.

Establishing Prices Using a Bottom-up Approach

In the break-even calculations provided above, the package prices were predetermined. However, it is necessary to be able to determine what price should be charged for a specific product based upon a company's costs of operation. It is not good enough to adopt a pricing structure based on "what the competitors use" or because "it sounds about right", since all businesses will vary in their investment structure, costs and profit expectations. Instead, adventure programmers should use a logical "bottom up" approach to establishing prices.

A bottom-up approach starts by calculating the desired profit and adding income taxes, management fees, fixed costs and variable costs to it. Once the total costs are determined, it is then a matter of dividing by the number of trips expected to be sold in order to establish a realistic trip price.

The bottom-up approach is comprised of the following steps:[1]

1. *Determine the desired profit by multiplying the desired rate of return by the owner's investment. For example, if the owner has invested $250,000 and requires a 15% return, this would be $37,500 ($250,000 x .15 = $37,500).*

2. *Determine the fixed expenses and management fees. This includes depreciation, marketing, interest paid, property taxes, insurance, loans and mortgages, rent and management fees (owner wages).*

3. *Determine the variable expenses. This includes guide wages, transportation, supplies and operations.*

4. *Total the three amounts above to establish the total costs. This is also the amount of revenue required to cover the total expenses and profit.*

5. *Determine the average trip price by dividing the revenue required by the number of trips expected to be sold.*

---

[1] *This is a simplified version of a complex process which would also include estimates of pre-tax income, undistributed operating expense, etc.*

Table 8-4 ❖ Bottom-up Pricing Approach for Wenatchee Trail Rides

Desired profit ($250,000 x .15 = $37,500) $37,500

Fixed Costs
Depreciation 30,000
Interest paid 90,000
Property taxes 25,000
Insurance..5,000
Marketing 40,000
Administration 30,000
Total fixed costs **$220,000**

Variable Costs
Guide wages 90,000
Transportation 35,000
Trip operations 125,000
Total variable costs..**$250,000**

Total costs..**$507,500**
(Divided by) Projected number of customers *575*
Required trip price ....**$ 882.60**

Table 8-4 is an example of the bottom-up pricing process for Wenatchee Trail Rides. Note that the desired profit, fixed costs and variable costs are combined to calculate the total costs to operate the business for the period. Once the total cost is established, it can then be divided by the projected number of customers in order to arrive at an appropriate trip price. For example, $507,500 divided by 575 customers equals $882.60. So, $882.60 is the minimum price that should be charged. However, any price above this would add profit to the business at a rate equal to the contribution margin per person.

In addition, by changing the price charged and dividing this into the total costs, you can calculate the number of customers you need to cover the costs.

Profit Margins

Business owners run their businesses with the objective of taking in more revenues than they pay out in expenses. An excess of total revenues over total expenses is called net income, net earnings or net profit. If total expenses are greater than total revenues, the result is called a net loss.

Table 8-5 ✤ Annapurna Circuit Trek — Nepal
Income Statement (in US$)

Variable Cost per Person for a Group of 10

Four nights in a Kathmandu hotel	$244
Two half-day van tours near Kathmandu	20
Flight to Pokhara	154
Airport transfers	18
Sherpa Sirdar wages: $12/day (no Western leader)	30
Wages for camp helpers and cooks ($6–$10/day)	135
Porters (30–40 x $5.50/day + insurance)	438
Equipment (amortized over 3 years)	65
Food	210
Kerosene ($4.00/gallon x 200 gallons)	68
Trash removal and recycling	25
Trekking fees	45
Contingency fund	25
Oxygen and Gamow Bag	48
Medical/Evacuation insurance	25
Total variable costs (per person)	**$1,550**

Fixed Costs per Person

North American office (rent, utilities, operating)	129
Kathmandu office	27
Pre-trip services (literature, advice, visa help)	209
Marketing expense	70
Travel agent and credit card commissions	95
Total fixed costs (per person)	**$530**

Total cost	**$2,080**
Price charged to customers	**$2,190**
Net income (profit margin) 5%	**$110**

a A Western leader would add $460 per person to the cost of the trip, while a Sherpa would add only $350.

b Assume that 1/4 of the clients come from travel agents; 3/4 use credit cards.

Generally, an income statement presents a summary of revenues and expenses for a specific period of business operations. It shows the net income position for the business' overall operations. In addition, income statements may be constructed for specific trips with the intent of showing the profit or loss position of the trip by itself. Table 8-5 shows a sample income statement for a Nepal trek on the Annapurna Circuit which has a contribution margin of $640

($2,190 charged per person minus $1,550 variable costs per person). This contribution margin includes a markup of 41.25% (36.25% applied towards fixed costs and 5% towards profit).

Table 8-6 ✧ The Profitability of Adventure Businesses

A 1996 study completed by America Outdoors on the profitability of adventure businesses in the United States analysed revenues and expenses for white-water rafting, canoe and kayak instruction, canoe rentals and similar companies. This study found that the average net income equalled 4.75% of all revenues and has done so for the past three years. Revenues from all profit centres such as trip fees, retail sales, rentals, campground and lodging, instruction, food and beverage were included. Total compensation to owners, partners and stockholders equalled 7.6% of total revenues.

Source: The Adventure Travel Business Magazine

Marketing Expenditures

As with the pricing of trip packages, the establishment of marketing budgets may be carried out in one of two manners: top down or bottom up. When using a top-down approach, the business manager would determine the amount of monies available for marketing, either by what has been spent in the past or what amount is expected to be left over, and spend this amount. Whether or not the amount is adequate or suitable is given less importance than what is available.

A bottom-up approach would consist of determining specifically where and how the business should market in order to achieve the level of sales desired. The costs of this plan would then be calculated, and the amount required to achieve the desired amount of marketing would be established and budgeted for.

Although the bottom-up approach to establishing a marketing budget is deemed the best, it is seldom carried out by adventure businesses. Establishing marketing budgets based upon "whatever we can afford" is rarely going to achieve the desired results.

For comparative purposes with other tourism businesses, a general, well-established guideline regarding marketing expenditures is to spend 10% of gross revenues on marketing when launching a new business or product, 7% of gross revenues when the business is established but desiring a relatively aggressive approach, and 5% of gross revenues when it is mature and attempting to maintain the product's position in the market.

Table 8-7 ✦ Mount Toubkal Trek — Morocco Income Statement (in US$)

Variable Cost per Person for a Group of 10

Three nights hotel accommodation $54
Ten nights camping accommodation 80
Two nights Berber family homestay 40
Medina tour 2
Porters and mules 50
Local guide..20
Western trip leader 50
Local transport 15
Insurance..55
Total variable costs (per person) **$366**

Price charged to customers **$896**

Contribution applied to fixed costs (140%) **$512**
Net income (profit margin — 5%) **$18**

The total contribution margin in this example is based on a markup of 145% (of which 140% is applied to fixed costs and 5% is intended as profit).

References

Garrison, R., et al. ***Managerial Accounting***. 3rd ed. Irwin Inc., 1996.

Horngren, et al. ***Financial Accounting***. 2nd Canadian ed. Prentice-Hall Canada Inc., 1991.

Lewis, R., et al. ***Marketing Leadership in Hospitality***. 2nd ed. Van Nostrand Reinhold, 1995.

McCarthy, et al. ***Basic Marketing***. 7th Canadian ed. Irwin Inc., 1994.

Morrison, A. ***Hospitality and Travel Marketing***. Delmar Publishers Inc., 1989.

Appendix

A

Business
Plan
Example
for
The
Adventure
Company

**Prepared by
David E. Kitzman
April 1995**

Author's Note

The following appendix is an example of a business plan which has been prepared for the hypothetical business entitled "The Adventure Company". As outlined in Chapter Six, a business plan is a living document which is intended to be updated and changed when required in order to target it towards a specific reader. The document included here was written with the intent of having it serve as both a business feasibility study for the writer and as a package to present to investors to attract the capital required to start the business.

The Executive Summary

Company Status

The Adventure Company was incorporated in the Province of British Columbia on March 12, 1995. The company has one appointed director, David Edward Kitzman. The company has been set up as a non-reporting company. Its share structure provides for 500,000 Class "A" shares (50,000 allotted to the director). Five hundred thousand Class "B" shares are available to investors (0 shares allotted).

The company is presently modifying its existing marketing plan to develop a comprehensive five-year marketing strategy for its sea-kayaking business.

Mission Statement

The Adventure Company's goal is to prosper and grow by providing an exceptional level of service to all clients through its friendly and highly trained staff. The company will promote environmental stewardship in a practical manner in all aspects of its operations.

Management

The Adventure Company is operated by David Kitzman (President). All company duties will be performed by Mr. Kitzman, including: formulation of policies, programming and staffing, marketing, financial strategies and risk management. Mr. Kitzman's background is very diversified and includes outdoor guiding skills and post-secondary education directly related to adventure tourism. Business, marketing and legal liability courses were part of the curriculum.

Product

The company's only product is high-quality kayak-touring trips using sea kayaks. Tours will be offered on many of B.C.'s southern interior lakes, with the main focus being Okanagan Lake. In addition to these trips, The Adventure Company will offer sea-kayaking trips to the Sea of Cortez near the Baja Peninsula, Mexico, in the winter and spring seasons.

Product Benefits

The Okanagan trips will provide clientele with an opportunity to discover the wonders of manoeuvring a touring kayak around the lake while at the same time enjoying scenic views from a perspective that many visitors to the Okanagan never experience. From the lake, access can be gained to many resorts, restaurants, parks, beaches and other local attractions. The company will offer a variety of trips including half-day introductory trips as well as one-, two- and three-day trips. One of our three-day trips will feature overnight accommodation at a guest house or bed-and-breakfast facility. This unique feature will appeal to many people who would be uncomfortable camping out.

Baja trips will be more traditional, featuring tent camping along the beaches. These trips will be seven days in length; high-quality food and services will be offered to clientele.

Market

Ocean kayaking has gained incredible popularity over the past five years. As with most outdoor activities, kayak touring has its own special appeal. Many people like the often relaxing effect of paddling a touring kayak. The opportunity to see plenty of wildlife and explore the shorelines is also another factor in the increasing popularity of this sport. As the coastal market has an abundance of kayak-touring companies, it is the intention of The Adventure Company to find a market niche: kayak touring on inland waters. The company will be using the growing popularity of the sport to enter the market, but will offer a unique service since very few companies offer kayak tours on B.C.'s interior lakes.

Competition

At present only one company is offering lake-touring trips in the Okanagan. Okanagan Kayaking[1] distributed brochures in 1994. A very limited number of its trips ran because it provided no other marketing for its product.

---

[1] *This name has been changed for the purposes of the demonstration plan.*

Financial Viability

This company's financial prospects look excellent. Only a small amount of start-up cash is required, and the company's projected net income is $17,000 in its first year of operation. The company will have capital assets of $45,000 (boats, accessories and office equipment). It will pay its president/director a salary of $30,000/year and will employ two to three other staff seasonally. The company is offering a product for which there is a continuously growing market, and the market niche selected works strongly in its favour. This will ensure that the sale of its product will increase in future years of operation. In its first-year financial analysis, the company's profit margin is projected at 11% as compared with an industry average of 6%. Return on investment is 25% compared with a 10% industry average. Overall, the profitability of the company looks excellent using the present assumptions and projections. *See "Financial Section" in the Business Plan.*

Financial Requirements

The Adventure Company needs financing for its initial acquisition of boats and office equipment. The required sum of $28,000 will go directly to the purchase of double sea-touring kayaks and necessary accessories. As outlined in the Business Plan, the company will be able to pay off this debt in five years.

The Business Plan

The Company

1. Company Overview

i. Origins

The Adventure Company was the inspiration of David Kitzman and was formulated as a marketing/business project while he attended the University College of the Cariboo. Today, the proof of the idea's validity is that "The Adventure Company" is now becoming a reality. The company's founder grew up in the Okanagan and had the opportunity to observe the expanding market of this area as a vacation destination. A desire to live and work in the area has prompted him to start The Adventure Company based out of Kelowna, B.C.

ii. Mission Statement

The Adventure Company's goal is to prosper and grow by providing an exceptional level of service to all clients through its friendly and highly trained staff. The company will promote environmental stewardship in a practical manner in all aspects of its operations.

iii. Objectives

Numerous recreational water activities are enjoyed in the Okanagan valley, which extends from Vernon in the north to Osoyoos in the south. Only one company offers guided kayak tours in the area or any type of instructional use of touring kayaks. There is still an excellent opportunity to enter the Okanagan market, and this is the niche that The Adventure Company intends to fill.

It is the intent of this company to offer high-quality, fun, lake kayak-touring in the Okanagan area. There are numerous opportunities to expand the services of this company to utilize the resources of local businesses. Several fine resorts, hotels, restaurants and bed-and-breakfast businesses are located on lakefront property or within close proximity to it. In addition, many bus tours pass through the Okanagan valley. These are all potential resources which, in addition, provide profitable areas of expansion for the company's services.

iv. Current Status

At present the company is in the beginning stages of development. It has been incorporated in the Province of B.C. as "The Adventure Company Inc." The company is now proceeding to initialize its place in the Okanagan valley. Manufacturers and suppliers of boats and other equipment essential to the operation are being contacted at this time. Information sheets and brochures will be distributed throughout western Canada. These sheets and brochures advertise half-, one-, two- and three-day Okanagan trips starting in January, 1996. A limited number of trips are being offered in the 1995 season mainly for promotional purposes. This will allow the company time to work on its marketing strategies for the 1996 season as well as to fine-tune its product delivery. Brochure designs for the 1996/97 season are being worked on now. Job positions will be advertised for one guide for winter 1996 and for a booking-and-enquiries receptionist for early spring 1996. Some of the initial start-up costs have been covered, but financing will be required for the purchase of boats and office equipment.

2. Organization of the Company

i. Legal and Financial Status
The Adventure Company is a limited company incorporated under the laws of the Province of British Columbia, with its registered office at:

> 123 Anywhere St., Kelowna, B.C.

Its officers and directors are:

> David Edward Kitzman, President and Secretary
> 123 Anywhere St., Kelowna, B.C.

There are presently no other officers or directors of The Adventure Company.

ii. Share Structure
This company is set up with 500,000 Class "A" voting shares, of which 50,000 have been allotted to the only director of the company (David Kitzman). The company has 500,000 Class "B" nonvoting shares available to investors.

iii. Management
The management hierarchy is set up with David Kitzman as President/Secretary; he is responsible for all aspects of the company operation.

iv. Roles
Mr. Kitzman assumes the position of President/Director and Secretary of this one-person company. He will also perform the duties of program and staffing manager; marketing, financing and risk management manager; and part-time guide. Mr. Kitzman's background is very diversified and is reflected in his present knowledge of business skills. During his formative years he was exposed to a small family business that is still owned and operated by his father. He had his first introduction to business courses while enrolled in the Automotive Service Technology Program at the Southern Alberta Institute of Technology. After many years of getting an inside look at how businesses operate while he worked as a licensed automotive technician, he

decided to move towards a new career path in the outdoor adventure industry. Five seasons working with Outward Bound have given him substantial insights into the guiding industry as well as a look at the financial and marketing skills required to successfully maintain a viable operation. He recently graduated from the University College of the Cariboo with a diploma from the Adventure Travel Guide Program. The Adventure Travel Guide Program consists of industry-standard outdoor adventure skills courses and certifications as well as academically oriented courses such as Tourism Marketing, Legal Liability, Risk Management, Accounting and Business of Adventure Tourism courses. Mr. Kitzman's background gives him an excellent advantage in his new venture as owner of The Adventure Company.

Other positions will be filled after extensive interviews with prospective employees. Positions to be filled include: booking-and-enquiries receptionist, guides and part-time staff as required.

v. Role Descriptions

President/Director: The President/Director is responsible for all financial, marketing and administrative concerns.

Booking-and-enquiries Receptionist: This important position will require a person who is exceptionally good at communicating with people and who has excellent organizational skills.

Guide: The guide's position is a challenging job which requires people skills, technical expertise, and considerable personal responsibility and decision making.

vi. Personnel Policies

This company will have written policies for all employees which will define all eventualities such as layoffs, termination, sick leave, grievance situations, discipline, holidays and working conditions as well as a policy outlining how they will be paid. All policies will be given to employees in an employee handbook.

vii. Contractors

In the event that work is contracted out to another guide or company, the contractor will have to sign a written Contractor Agreement with The Adventure Company. *See Attachment A, Contractor Agreement.*

3. Strategy for the Future

i. Where Is the Company Going?

The Company's long-term goal is to become a viable, well-known operation in British Columbia, recognized the world over for its excellence in providing high-quality trips with friendly, knowledgeable staff. It will expand the program base to offer trips in the Okanagan valley and the Kootenays, along the Pacific Coast from Victoria, B.C., to Anchorage, Alaska, and off the Baja Peninsula in Mexico. Private specialty trips will be organized to various world destinations for selective clientele interested in more extensive travel. These trips will be individually tailored to the interests of the clientele. European clientele will be sought after through aggressive marketing techniques in order to create a global client base for the company. This will also help ensure that all trips are filled to capacity and will create a list of clients who are more likely to book trips with the company in upcoming years. The Adventure Company will operate all trips under a policy of environmentally friendly guidelines, specific to each area of usage. The company will involve itself in local community projects and will hire as many local people as possible. Ten to fifteen people will be hired at its peak. The Adventure Company will be a name synonymous with "quality and fun adventure trips!"

ii. Company Strategy

Initially, the company will target the local market through the use of flyers, information sheets and brochures. It will handle its own marketing functions and will work on making contact with as many travel agencies as possible. The goal is to find an agency the company can work with to sell its trips. The local tourism association will be utilized for help with local marketing strategies. The Adventure Company will establish itself in the Okanagan and will then work on expanding its market to include a worldwide client base. Booth space in trade shows and conventions for wholesalers will be actively sought out to position this company favourably for a world market. A five-year marketing action plan will be followed to channel money for this purpose. This plan will encompass packaging, positioning, advertising, promotions and pricing strategies. An ongoing marketing evaluation will be implemented to improve and modify existing strategies. Some of this evaluation will be monitored through the tracking of customer enquiries. This will determine which methods of advertising are bringing in the greatest numbers of enquiries and bookings.

Excellent customer service will be vital in ensuring this company's potential to grow and expand. All staff will receive training which focuses on the company's philosophy and its commitment to providing this type of service. Continual monitoring of all aspects of the company, including feedback from customers and outside resources, along with an ability to change areas that need improvement, will allow this company to reach its long-term goals.

The company will use supporting professional services when necessary to ensure that it is operating productively. Services that might be used include those of professional accountants, lawyers, advertising agencies, market research firms, business consulting firms, bankers and other business associates.

The Product

1. Product Description

The Adventure Company will offer guided half-, one-, two- and three-day trips on Okanagan Lake and seven-day trips on the Sea of Cortez near the Baja Peninsula. The Okanagan trips will offer lakefront accommodations for some overnight trips and camping for others. The one-day sightseeing trips will start at 9 a.m. on Okanagan, Kalamalka or Shuswap Lake. The tour will start with an introduction to kayak touring and a demonstration by the guide of a wet exit and an Eskimo roll. Basic paddle strokes will be practised, and then the tour will start by moving along the shoreline before crossing the lake and stopping at a lunch site. After lunch the group will continue exploring the shoreline and will again cross the lake and finish the circuit at 3 p.m. This will be a typical itinerary for all one-day trips regardless of which lake the trip is on. Each lake trip will have different local attractions to be explored and activities to take part in. Some of the possibilities will be: swimming, short hikes, fruit picking from local orchards, orchard tours, searching for the Ogopogo, and fishing. This type of trip will offer people an opportunity to paddle on the lake and then enjoy the comforts of home. The company will also be offering instructional kayak workshops with the intent of attracting clientele interested in ocean-kayaking trips. These workshops will help the company increase its client list and generate potential clients for ocean trips in the Baja. The Baja trips will be offered in the spring and fall and will include all meals and tent accommodation.

2. Positioning

The product provided will be oriented towards customer satisfaction. Any staff hired will have to be knowledgeable of the area they are working in. A professional attitude and neat appearance on the part of staff will be important. A well-organized schedule will also help maintain a positive image for the company. Most customers will be new to the area and will be asking questions concerning local history and the availability of services, etc. Their first impression of the company as helpful and knowledgeable will provide a positive image both to other customers and to the community. Our position in the market will be to offer high-quality trips at prices comparable to those of coastal kayak companies.

Quality service and comparable pricing will help the company capture a greater share of the market, while positive "word of mouth" advertising from satisfied clients increases future sales. Starting the company in a position of higher quality and moderately high prices (*see chart A-1*) will give it the appearance of being a well-established business. This will attract more clients because they will feel more secure about booking a trip with the company. With high-quality service and a high standard of care for its clients, The Adventure Company can focus on

Chart A-1 ✧ The Adventure Company Product Position

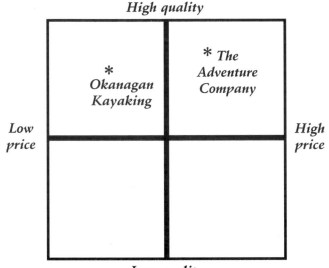

maintaining rather than worry about increasing its positioning in the market.

By starting in this position, the company will be forced to ensure that the entire operation has been thoroughly planned.

3. Market Needs for the Product

A large percentage of Okanagan tourists are 35 to 54 years of age; this market will be targeted by the company. This age group may not be interested in more physically strenuous activities such as water-skiing, windsurfing or mountain biking. However, sea kayaking is looked upon as a sport that is not overly strenuous, and people can easily learn the skills needed to propel the craft in less than one hour. Prospective clients will also feel that travelling on an inland lake in warmer waters will be safer than being on the ocean, and this may allow them to try a sport they might not otherwise feel confident enough to do. This age group has a high disposable income; this means they would be willing to spend more money on a trip if they felt it met their interests.

A large portion of Okanagan Lake's shoreline is commercially or privately owned, leaving few areas open for people who want to camp. However, these people would still like to travel on the lake. This gives The Adventure Company an opportunity to cater to them by offering tours with pre-arranged sleeping accommodations, a unique product that is not presently offered on the lake. There is one business that has just started to market kayak trips on

Okanagan Lake as of March 1994. Sea Kayaks[2] in Summerland, B.C., has a kayak manufacturing business and has just introduced a brochure outlining trips it intends to offer under the name Okanagan Kayaking. At present it is proposing to offer single- and multi-day trips on Okanagan Lake only. This still leaves the market open for trips on other lakes such as Kalamalka and Shuswap lakes.

The Market

1. Market Statistics

i. Size of Market

According to a 1989 Marine Tourism study in B.C., 75% of West Coast kayaking clients came from Canada and 48% of these clients were from B.C. A comparison of statistics has been made using the 1989 B.C. Marine Survey and the 1991 B.C. Resident Travel Survey (prepared by *Canadian Fact* in January, 1992). The comparison shows the similarities in ages between clients participating in sea-kayaking trips and B.C. resident travellers.

Chart A-2 ❖ Age Comparison of B.C. Resident Travellers and B.C. Coastal Kayakers

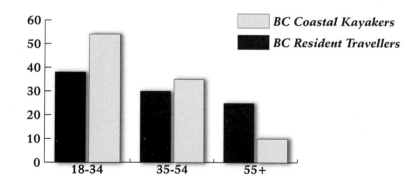

These statistics show that the group between 18 and 34 years of age is the best group to target for the West Coast market. However, while travelling in the Okanagan, this age group would be inclined to participate in more active water sports than lake kayaking. For this reason the company would target members of the 35–54 and 55+ age groups, who would enjoy stops at resorts and attractions. These two age groups represent 62% of B.C. resident travellers and 47% of coastal kayakers, a sizeable portion of the potential market. This does not eliminate the 18- to 34-year-old market group, since some of the people in this group will be interested in

---

[2] *This name has been changed for the purposes of the demonstration plan.*

shorter, half-day trips if they have never kayaked before. Chart A-3 presents another set of statistics concerning coastal kayakers:

Chart A-3 ❖ B.C. Coastal Kayakers

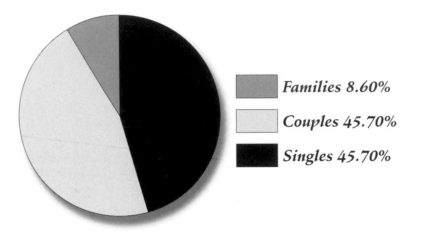

Families 8.60%

Couples 45.70%

Singles 45.70%

Since there is an even split between couples and singles, it can be assumed that there will be an equal opportunity to attract both of these target groups. Although the initial target market is made up of the tourists travelling through the central Okanagan, the company uses a statistical analysis of Lower Mainland and Vancouver Island kayak operators in order to establish an effective marketing strategy.

ii. Rate of Growth

The recent increase in population throughout the entire Okanagan valley has created greater market potential for adventure companies. Silver Star Mountain Resort is a good example of a company taking advantage of the popularity of the area's outdoor activities. Because of the large population in the Okanagan valley and the influx of tourists during the summer months, the resort has recently been offering mountain bike tours on the ski hill during the summer. There will certainly be many more companies offering outdoor activities in the future as soon as the potential market is realized.

Sea kayaking statistics from 1989 stated that there were 15 companies on the West Coast of B.C. in 1989. There are now approximately 125 kayak operations, including rental services, in the same area. This substantial increase in the number of operators reflects an increase in the number of consumers buying the product.

iii. Purchasing Characteristics of the Target Market

Okanagan Lake is one of the main attractions of the Okanagan valley, so it makes sense that water sport activities have major appeal. Some of the water sports on the lake are scuba diving, canoeing, swimming, windsurfing and rentals of power boats for water-skiing, tubing, fishing and sightseeing.

Kayak touring has seen an incredible increase in the numbers of participants over the last 10 years. Some of the reasons for this are:

❖ more awareness that the sport exists (this may be from word of mouth or promotional advertising)

❖ promotion of kayak touring as a safe sport due to stringent industry standards

❖ easier access to appropriate equipment, whether renting or buying

❖ higher-quality equipment which makes it easier to learn and become proficient at this activity

❖ a steady increase in the number of people wanting an outdoor experience as part of their holiday

Traditional outdoor experiences such as hiking and backpacking are still popular, but now many people are looking for something new and exciting. Kayak touring has become one of the alternative outdoor experiences available.

2. Company Perspectives on the Market

i. Product Line

Lake kayak-touring is a product unique to the interior regions of British Columbia. Although paddling is an attraction in itself, The Adventure Company trips will have numerous points of interest mapped out which will appeal to a broad range of customers. A destination will be marketed as part of the kayaking experience, for example, Okanagan Mountain Park, so that participants will gain a sense of achievement from the experience even if they take part in a short day trip. All trips will include basic paddling and safety instruction. An instructional course on ocean-kayaking skills and safety will be offered to attract customers who are interested in ocean kayaking but do not have the time to take a preliminary instructional course on the ocean.

The Adventure Company will offer kayak-touring trips on Okanagan and Kalamalka lakes. We will tour on the lakes and then stop at lakefront accommodation or camping sites for overnight trips. The trips will cater to clients who want a paddling experience which is shorter and less intimidating than an ocean trip or is closer to their travel destination. As well, our clients will be able to enjoy the comforts of a soft bed at the end of the day and an opportunity to go out to a restaurant for dinner. There are also many attractions throughout the valley which would be of interest to visitors. This is a new concept for guided touring of Okanagan Lake and will appeal to many people. Other programs offered will be overnight trips using provincial parks, forestry campsites and private land as camping areas for our clients, and day trips which will include stops at scenic locations and a picnic-style lunch. Day trips will be offered on Okanagan, Kalamalka and Shuswap lakes. A more traditional trip offered will be a seven-day ocean kayaking trip to the Baja Peninsula. Guests will stay in tents and meals will be provided for them. This will provide the company with an opportunity to use the equipment purchased and to generate cash flow in the Okanagan's off-season.

The Adventure Company has only one competitor in the Okanagan at the present time for the type of trip it is offering. A market does exist for this type of trip because many people who have moved to the Okanagan will seek out an adventurous activity to participate in. It is already a popular area for water sports, and this type of trip will provide more variety and will fill the gap between action water sports and the power boat tours.

This company's intentions are to market this product to clients with a higher disposable income as well as to clients who are willing to camp out. Above all, the goal is to cater to clients who want the personal satisfaction of touring the lake using a very unique form of transportation.

ii. Market Trends

In the future The Adventure Company will target the European market. It is also the intention to obtain contracts with local hotels and resorts in order to offer package deals for their customers. Bus tours which travel through the valley will also be a target, as the company could offer them half-day paddling excursions.

Due to the technological advances in boat and paddle designs, it is becoming easier for people to learn the sport of sea kayaking. Lighter materials such as kevlar and fibreglass are being used for boats and paddles, making travel on the water less strenuous and the boats easier to control. As with many other sports such as cross-country skiing and mountain biking, sea kayaking is still gaining in popularity with people of all ages. The market will continue to grow for all types of adventure sports in the future, since adventure activities have become a focus of many people during their weekends and holidays. More people are being introduced to adventure activities, including sea kayaking, so there will be a need for introductory-type trips as well as more challenging trips for experienced paddlers. Due to the increased awareness of and interest in adventure activities, a greater demand will be placed on existing adventure companies and more opportunities will be available for new companies. The trend in recent years has been for companies to operate in ways which help preserve the environment and to be culturally sensitive to local people within the operating area. This environmental and cultural awareness will continue to be an issue for people planning their holidays. It is important for all businesses in the adventure travel industry to have a genuine concern for these issues and to institute company policies and training in order to ensure that company practices meet or exceed the public's expectations.

3. Reaction to Market

i. Introduction Difficulties

Some of the difficulties in introducing this product are:

❖ making the company visible and well known in the area

❖ ensuring the target market is reached

❖ establishing contracts with local hotels and businesses to increase sales and awareness of the company

Competition

1. Overview

There is only one competitor in the Okanagan/Shuswap area for the type of trips The Adventure Company is offering. Okanagan Kayaking in Summerland, B.C., has started to market trips on Okanagan Lake using sea kayaks. It also offers a boat rental service. The company is operated by the owners of Sea Kayaks Ltd., a sea-kayak manufacturing business. Boat rentals are available from other businesses, but only open-cockpit touring kayaks are rented at Sports Rent in Kelowna. At Spirit Pond Rentals in Sicamous, sea-touring kayaks are rented by the day only.

Okanagan Kayaking distributed brochures in 1994 but did not use any other marketing techniques to market its trips. The company said it was not aggressively pursuing clients. A new brochure is being printed for 1995 but will not be available for distribution until May 1995. It was hinted that these trips would be marketed more aggressively this year. Okanagan Kayaking is presently looking to hire someone to act as a showroom salesperson and a kayaking guide. This indicates that it is not sure it will fill its advertised trips. It is starting to market these trips very late in the season and will be relying on the influx of tourists to fill them. The company's success will depend on the other marketing promotions it uses in addition to its brochures.

Competition with other water sports is high, with every sport from power boating, scuba diving, sailing, water-skiing, parasailing on water skis and windsurfing being offered in the area. However, the fact that a large number of people are attracted to the Okanagan for these other sport activities can only benefit The Adventure Company by providing a source of potential customers. This gives us an opportunity to offer an activity which is easier to participate in than most of the other activities mentioned.

A comparison of trip prices is shown here using some popular coastal kayaking companies and the only local competition, Okanagan Kayaking. Along with financial projections for The Adventure Company, this competition price comparison will provide The Adventure Company with a basis for its own competitive pricing strategy. All trips listed below were found in colour brochures ranging from single-sheet card stock to multi-page books. Prices were generally always listed. Trips include food and necessary equipment, unless noted.

2. Competition Prices

Ecosummer Expeditions .... *1995 Pricing (CAN$)*
7 days, Sea Kayaking (Baja Peninsula) $1,360
5 days, Sea Kayaking (Gulf Islands) $625
2 days, Intro. to Sea Kayaking $245
8 days, Bowron Lakes (canoe trip) $1,245

Northern Lights Expeditions .... *1995 Pricing*
6 days, Sea Kayaking (Port McNeill) $1,235

Geoff Evans Kayak Center
1 day, Kayak Introduction, (Cultus Lake) $75
2 days, Sea Kayak Intro. Weekend (Cultus Lake) $175
3 days, Clinic/Cruise on Cultus Lake and Fraser River $250

Tofino Expeditions .... *1995 Pricing*
6 days, Sea Kayaking, (Clayoquot Sound) $850

Outside Expeditions (East Coast) .... *1995 Pricing*
3 days, Coastlines and Country Inns $590
3 days, Murray Harbour and Eastern Shores $390
6 days, Cape Breton Highlands $770

Okanagan Kayaking, Summerland, B.C. .... *1994 Pricing*
1 day, Introductory Lesson (Okanagan Lake) $65
2 days, Lake Tour $175
3 days, Lake Tour $300

Sports Rent, Kelowna .... *1994 Pricing*
Lake kayaks (contoured, open cockpit) $20/day

Spirit Pond, Sicamous ....*1994 Pricing*
Single sea kayak $45/day

Pricing for The Adventure Company trips is based on a financial forecast which assumes a client enrolment of between 33% and 100%, depending on the trip length (maximum enrolment is six clients per trip for Okanagan trips and ten clients for Baja trips).

The Adventure Company ⬧ 1996 Pricing

1/2-day Introduction to Lake Kayaking plus Short Tour ....$40/pers.
1-day Okanagan Lake Sightseeing Trip...$75/pers.
1-day Kalamalka Lake Sightseeing Trip..$75/pers.
2-day Weekend Introduction to Paddling and Camping ....$75/pers.
3-day Okanagan Lake Tour (tent camping) ....$400/pers.
3-day Okanagan Lake Tour (guesthouse accommodation) ....$550/pers.
7-day Baja (Sea of Cortez) Tour (tent camping) ....$1400/pers.

Sales and Marketing

1. Advertising and Promotion

The Adventure Company will start marketing its product seven to eight months in advance of its trip dates. Initially, brochures will be the first item to be distributed. One strategy will be to obtain mailing lists from other companies which have clientele actively seeking adventure trips. Establishing contacts within the industry will also be beneficial to gaining access to wholesalers willing to take on new clients. A new marketing tool exists in the form of the Internet. Many businesses are now advertising their products on this worldwide communication network. This is an excellent opportunity for free global advertising. Some of the limitations of the Internet are: the relatively low number of people who know how to access the system compared to the population base, and the fact that the target market of adventure seekers would have to be actively seeking information on the Internet. However, the continued increase in awareness of the Internet will make advertising on it another option to consider when marketing trips.

i. Introduction Difficulties
a) Visibility
Advertising will be important in order to create recognition of the product. A promotional trip will be organized for owners of local businesses that The Adventure Company will be dealing

with, as well as the local media. It is hoped that this will help create more awareness of the company and also get an article written for a special-interest section in the local (Okanagan) newspaper's Sunday edition. Ideally, the article will outline the company's services including details of trips offered and will feature pictures of staff and boats. Local radio stations will be asked to advertise the "Grand Opening" event for the company and also to participate in a live broadcast from the shores of Okanagan Lake, where short but free rides will be offered to the public. The Chamber of Commerce, travel information booths and local businesses will be plugged with brochures and posters. Brochures will also be sent to selected businesses throughout B.C., Alberta and Washington. To increase visibility within the local operating area, all staff will be given T-shirts to wear with the company name and logo on them. All boats and the company van will have the company name painted on them.

b) Reaching the Target Market

Our initial target market will be people 35 and over. A large portion of this market will be vacationers travelling through the area, including a large number of seniors who may be travelling on bus tours. According to a 1985 National Tour Foundation survey, 60% of group tour passengers were female, single and 51 to 72 years of age. To target this group, we will advertise our product in seniors' magazines and will post information bulletins in businesses frequented by seniors. Part of our marketing process will be to promote our service to tour operators that frequently come through the Okanagan/Shuswap area. We will include a description of our service in a package with other local businesses or custom tailor it with an existing bus tour package. This will provide us with greater exposure to our target market, since our product will be marketed nationally by the tour operators and wholesalers. The company name may not be advertised, but once the clients have taken a trip with us the company name will receive more exposure nationally. An attempt will be made to generate as much public awareness as possible through all possible channels of advertising media. The best advertising will be word of mouth, but it will be a number of years before there has been a large enough number of clients on trips to see any effect from this. Direct mail will be a consideration if a mailing list is obtained, but will not otherwise be considered due to the high cost involved.

c) Establishing Sales Contacts

In addition to targeting bus tours, The Adventure Company will promote its product to local businesses. Package deals will be worked out with hotels to provide half-day paddling tours which finish with either a lunch or a dinner catered by the hotel. Package deals will be offered to companies for their employees and also for people involved in conventions. In order to be successful in obtaining these types of accounts, a complete presentation package will be set up which will be individually tailored to the type of organization The Adventure Company is targeting.

Company Operations

1. Product Packaging

i. Facilities

This company will lease its office and storage space from David Kitzman. The space will be the site for its registered and records office and for the storage of equipment and boats. The operation will, however, be mobile. A van and trailer for hauling boats and equipment will allow it to be self-sufficient. All trips will start from public access points on the lake or from private facilities if access can be arranged. The company will use a house which is in an area zoned for commercial use. This will allow it to be converted into an office and will also provide rooms for guides to stay in if they do not live in the area. A section of the house will be used for gear, equipment and boat storage. The kitchen will be utilized by guides for personal use and for preparation of trip food including baked goods. The office will include a computer system, photocopier, fax/answering machine and appropriate office furniture.

ii. Equipment

The operation will require a substantial amount of gear and equipment. The following lists will describe the necessary equipment for each section of the operation including office supplies and equipment, boats and accessories, vehicles, safety equipment and kitchen appliances.

Office

Two desks, 3 chairs, 1 computer system with colour laser printer, software such as Micro Soft Office, 1 fax/answering machine, 1 photocopier, 1 multi-line phone, copy paper and other stationary, accounting journals and ledgers, company minute book, bookshelves and miscellaneous office supplies.

Boats

Six double kayaks, 3 single kayaks, 15 spray skirts, 15 paddles, 9 bailing pumps, 15 PFDs, 70 metres of accessory cord, 15 paddling jackets, 8 emergency signalling kits, 1 repair kit, 15 ten-litre dry bags, 15 rain hats.

Vehicle/Trailer

One 15-passenger van with trailer hitch, 1 boat trailer with a capacity to hold 10 to 12 boats, tie-down straps, fire extinguisher, first-aid kit, roadside emergency kit, axe.

Safety Equipment
Two fire extinguishers, 5 first aid kits, 2 guide towlines.

iii. Trip Preparation

All initial preparation for Okanagan trips will be done at the boat and equipment storage site. This will include preparing boats and equipment, preparing food for trips that include a picnic lunch and preparing food for overnight trips. Food will be prepared the evening before the trip. Picnic lunches will typically include a variety of fresh locally grown fruit, fruit salad, fresh whole grain bread, speciality cheeses, deli-made sandwich spreads, garden-fresh vegetables and dips, and juice products.

The guide or guides on day programs will be responsible for all aspects of the trip including checking the number of participating clients and arranging a meeting place in order to transport the clients to the boat launch site.

iv. Qualified Staff

In order to find qualified staff, job postings will be placed with organizations and associations where suitable people may be found, i.e. University College of the Cariboo (Adventure Guide Program), University of Calgary (Outdoor Pursuits Program) and Capilano College Outdoor Recreation Program. As mentioned in the section "The Company" under the heading Strategy for the Future, The Adventure Company will try to hire local people from within the Okanagan region first and from within B.C. second. Minimum qualifications will be adhered to when hiring guides. All guides will take a training course designed by The Adventure Company. The purpose of the training will be to ensure that all staff understand the Mission Statement and have the ability to provide the quality of service that is being advertised by the company.

Financial Forecast

Financial Assumptions

The following documentation is based on assumptions which include:

❖ *Number of trips offered*

❖ *Client capacity*

❖ *Availability of funding for capital expenditures*

❖ *A 14% interest rate over five years*

❖ *Pre-1996 marketing costs have been paid for with investor money*

All cash flow projections are based as accurately as possible on actual costs of products and services and on the projected requirements for these products and services.

The amount of start-up cash needed is based on the cost of equipment required and on the assumption that the company has already started to market its trips for the 1995 season. This pre-start-up marketing strategy will allow the company to operate with minimal start-up cash and will require only a relatively small loan from a lending institution. The financial risk to the lending institution will be minimal because the amount of the loan will be only 60% of the capital assets. The remainder of the start-up cash will be supplied by David Kitzman (the company president). If the company defaults on its loan in the first two years of operation, the lender could still easily recover its money since the value of the boats would be well above the value of the loan. As well, the term of the loan will be very short (five years). Due to the quality of the boats purchased, their value will still be very high at the end of the five-year loan period.

The following documentation shows that this company is a potentially viable operation able to generate enough revenue to sustain itself with only a minimal loan requirement.

The Adventure Company is seeking a $28,000 loan with a five-year term.

The Adventure Company Inc.
Pro Forma Opening Balance Sheet
Year Beginning January 1, 1996

Assets

Current Assets

Cash 0

Common shares 500

*Total current assets **$500***

Capital Assets

Office equipment / Misc. equipment (inc. GST) 3,504

Boats and equipment (inc. GST) 43,625

Repair tools (incl. GST) 871

*Total capital assets **$48,000***

*Total assets..**$48,500***

Liabilities and Stockholders' Equities

Liabilities

Note payable to D. Kitzman...20,000

Note payable to bank..28,000

*Total liabilities **$48,000***

Stockholders' Equity

Contributed capital, common shares 500

(50,000 Class "A" shares at $ 0.01 ea.)

*Total stockholders' equity **$500***

*Total liabilities and stockholders' equity **$48,500***

The Adventure Company Inc.

Pro Forma Income Statement
for the Year Ended December 31, 1996

Sales of Okanagan and Baja trips..**$156,260**

Cost of Goods Sold
Variable Trip Costs
Okanagan (food and gas)...7,508
Baja (food and gas)...18,000
Wages: Guides..27,300
Promotion...1,000
Travel   600
Total cost of goods sold **$54,408**

Gross profit[1] **$101,852**
Selling and administrative expense **$75,694**
Operating profit...**$26,158**

Net income before taxes $26,158
Taxes (33%)..$8,632

Net income **$17,526**

[1] *Includes $5,920 interest expense on notes payable*

The Adventure Company Inc.
Pro Forma Balance Sheet
as of December 31, 1996

Assets

Current Assets
Cash   33,413
(Less income tax) 8,632
Equals 24,781
Prepaid expenses (vehicle insurance) 500
Total current assets **$25,281**

Capital Assets
Office equipment / Misc. equipment..4,475
Boats and equipment 40,770
Office supplies..200
Total capital assets **$45,445**

Total assets...**$70,726**

Liabilities and Stockholders' Equity

Liabilities
GST payable 7,688
Accumulated amortization 4,524
Note payable to D. Kitzman..16,724
Note payable to bank...23,764
Total liabilities **$52,700**

Stockholders' Equity
Retained earnings...17,526
Contributed capital, common shares 500
(50,000 Class "A" shares at $ 0.01 ea.)
Total stockholders' equity...**$18,026**

Total liabilities and stockholders' equity **$70,726**

Break-even Chart

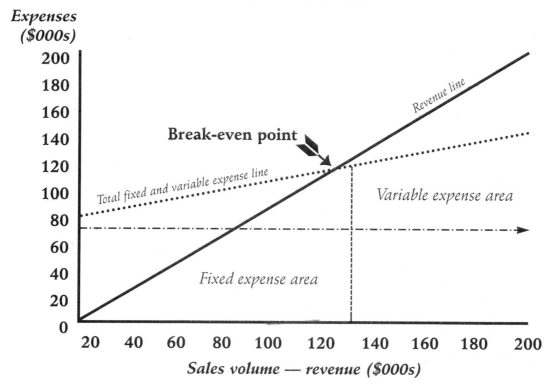

Expenses ($000s)

Break-even point

Total fixed and variable expense line

Revenue line

Variable expense area

Fixed expense area

Sales volume — revenue ($000s)

The Adventure Company Inc.
Condensed Income Statement

Total trip revenue $156,260

Expenses
Fixed expenses (administrative) 75,694
Variable expenses (cost of goods sold) 54,408
Total expenses $130,102

Net profit before taxes $26,158

Financial Analysis

		The Adventure Company	Industry Average
Profitability Ratios			
Profit margin =	$\dfrac{\text{Net income}}{\text{Sales}}$	$\dfrac{\$17{,}526}{156{,}260} = 11\%$	2%
Return on investment =	$\dfrac{\text{Net income}}{\text{Total assets}}$	$\dfrac{\$17{,}526}{70{,}726} = 25\%$	13%
Return on equity =	$\dfrac{\text{Net income}}{\text{Stockholders' equity}}$	$\dfrac{\$17{,}526}{18{,}026} = 97\%$	75%
Liquidity Ratios			
Current ratio =	$\dfrac{\text{Current assets}}{\text{Current liabilities}}$	$\dfrac{\$25{,}281}{\$12{,}212} = 2.07$	1%
Debt Utilization Ratios			
Debt to total assets =	$\dfrac{\text{Total debt}}{\text{Total assets}}$	$\dfrac{\$52{,}700}{\$70{,}726} = 75\%$	125%

Notes: 1) All information for financial analysis is based on figures taken from first-year balance sheet and income statements.

2) The "industry average" is based on real, but very limited data.

The Adventure Company ✦ Cash Flow Statement 1996

	January	February	March	April	May	June	July	August	September	October	November	December	Totals
Summary													
Cash on hand	6,734	19,343	24,522	27,801	21,450	14,426	17,418	22,910	17,709	12,558	18,937	33,413	
Total receipts	63,480	29,960	14,980	14,980	4,815	1,392	21,272	19,880	980		14,000	29,960	215,699
Total disbursements	56,746	17,351	9,801	11,701	11,166	8,416	18,280	14,388	6,181	5,151	7,621	15,484	182,286
Total cash flow	6,734	12,609	5,179	3,279	-6,351	-7,024	2,992	5,492	-5,201	-5,151	6,379	14,476	33,413
Ending balance	6,734	19,343	24,522	27,801	21,450	14,426	17,418	22,910	17,709	12,558	18,937	33,413	237,221
Opening balance	0	6,734	19,343	24,522	27,801	21,450	14,426	17,418	22,910	17,709	12,558	18,937	33,413
Receipts													
Cash sales (Okanagan)					4,500		19,880	19,880					44,260
Cash sales (Baja)	14,000	28,000	14,000	14,000							14,000	28,000	112,000
Loans and share capital	48,500												48,500
Other (GST collected)	980	1,960	980	980	315	1,392	1,392		980			1,960	10,939
Disbursements													
Boats/Accessories	44,045												44,045
Equipment/Supplies	100	100	100	100	100	100	100	100	100	100	100	100	1,200
Advertising/Brochures		5,000		500			3,000	500	500	500			10,000
Promotional expense					500						500		1,000
Office supplies / Postage	100	100	100	100	100	100	100	100	100	100	100	100	1,200
Wages, net (staff)	500												500
Prof. fees: (lawyer)			100			100	100		100		50		450
Repairs (general)					100	100	100	100	100				500
Licences/Fees/Dues	200												200
Travel expenses	50	50	50	50	50	50	50	50	50	50	50	50	600
Rent/Mortgage	600	600	600	600	600	600	600	600	600	600	600	600	7,200
Wages, gross (guides)					1,200	1,200	1,200	1,200	1,200	1,200			7,200
Wages, gross (office staff)	1,600	3,200	1,600	1,600		2,650	5,925	5,925			1,600	3,200	27,300
Insurance (liability)	2,500												2,500
Insur. (vehicle/trailer)				1,500									1,500
Insur.(building/contents)	1,000												1,000
Telephone	200	200	200	200	200	200	200	200	200	200	200	200	2,400
Utilities	150	150	150	150	150	150	150	150	150	150	150	150	1,800
GST paid for purchases	271	271	271	271	271	271	271	271	271	271	271	270	3,251
Loan payment A						2,638						2,638	5,276
Loan payment B	680	680	680	680	680	680	680	680	680	680	680	676	8,156
Management salary	2,500	2,500	2,500	2,500	2,500	2,500	2,500	2,500	2,500	2,500	2,500	2,500	30,000
Okanagan trip costs						600	3,454	3,454					7,508
Baja trip costs	2,250	4,500	2,250	2,250							2,250	4,500	18,000

The Adventure Company ❖ Cash Flow Statement 1997

Summary

Summary	January	February	March	April	May	June	July	August	September	October	November	December	Totals
Cash on Hand	25,281	27,714	40,477	44,491	47,924	41,727	38,744	44,543	52,842	46,476	41,479	48,012	$499,710
Total Receipts	14,980	29,960	14,980	14,980		7,383	23,925	23,925			14,980	29,960	175,073
Total Disbursements	12,547	17,197	10,966	11,547	6,197	10,366	18,126	15,626	6,366	4,997	8,447	14,012	136,394
Total Cash Flow	2,433	12,763	4,014	3,433	-6,197	-2,983	5,799	8,299	-6,366	-4,997	6,533	15,948	38,679
Ending Balance	27,714	40,477	44,491	47,924	41,727	38,744	44,543	52,842	46,476	41,479	48,012	63,960	538,389
Opening Balance	25,281	27,714	40,477	44,491	47,924	41,727	38,744	44,543	52,842	46,476	41,479	48,012	63,960

Receipts

Receipts	January	February	March	April	May	June	July	August	September	October	November	December	Totals
Cash Sales (Okanagan)						6,900	22,360	22,360					51,620
Cash Sales (Baja)	14,000	28,000	14,000	14,000							14,000	28,000	112,000
Loans & Share Capital													
Other (GST collected)	980	1,960	980	980		483	1,565	1,565			980	1,960	11,453

Disbursements

Disbursements	January	February	March	April	May	June	July	August	September	October	November	December	Totals
Boats/Accessories	100	100	100	100	100	100	100	100	100	100	100	100	1,200
Equipment/Supplies		5000		500			3000	500	500	500			10,000
Advertising/Brochures			500	500									1,000
Promotional Expense					500								1,200
Office Supplies/Postage	100	100	100	100	100	100	100	100	100	100	100	100	500
Prof. Fees: (Accountant)	500		100			100					100		450
Repairs (General)								50					200
Licenses/Fees/Dues	200												600
Travel Expenses	50	50	50	50	50	50	50	50	50	50	50	50	600
Rent/Mortgage	600	600	600	600	600	600	600	600	600	600	600	600	7,200
Wages, Gross (Office Staff)	1600	3200	1600	1600	1200	1200	1200	1200			1600	3200	27,300
Wages, Gross (Guides)	2500					2650	5925	5925					2,500
Insurance (Liability)													1,500
Insur. (Vehicle/Trailer)				1500									1,000
Insur.(Building/Contents)	1000												2,400
Telephone	200	200	200	200	200	200	200	200	200	200	200	200	2,400
Utilities	150	150	150	150	150	150	150	150	150	150	150	150	1,800
GST paid for purchases	117	117	117	117	117	117	117	117	117	117	117	117	1,404
Loan Payment "A"	680	680	680	680	680	680	680	680	680	680	680	676	5,276
Loan Payment "B"	2500	2500	2500	2500	2500	2500	2500	2500	2500	2500	2500	2500	8,156
Management Salary	2500	2500	2500	2500	2500	2500	2500	2500	2500	2500	2500	2500	30,000
Okanagan Trip Costs						600	3454	3454					7,508
Baja Trip Costs	2250	4500	2250	2250							2250	4500	18,000

Trip Pricing and Client Capacity Assumptions

Okanagan Trips

	June	July	August	Capacity[1]	Clients	Trip Price	Revenue
1/2-day	30 trips	31 trips	31 trips	33%	184	$40	$7,360
1-day		16 trips	16 trips	50%	96	$75	$7,200
Weekend	2 trips	4 trips	4 trips	100%	60	$175	$10,500
3-day		4 trips	4 trips	100%	48	$400	$19,200

Total number of clients 388   Total revenue $44,260

1 Percentage capacity rating based on 6 clients per trip

Seven-day Baja Trips

Months	Trips	Clients	Trip Price	Revenue
January	1	10	$1,400	$14,000
February	2	20	$1,400	$28,000
March	1	10	$1,400	$14,000
April	1	10	$1,400	$14,000
November	1	10	$1,400	$14,000
December	2	20	$1,400	$28,000
Total	**8**	**80**		**$112,000**

1997 Assumptions

❖ Trips and pricing will remain the same as in 1996.
❖ Client capacity will increase to 66% for Okanagan 1/2-day trips.
❖ Revenue for Okanagan trips will increase by $14,270.
❖ Baja trips will remain the same as in 1996.

Expenses
1996 Start-up Expenditures
(boat and office equipment)

Boats and Equipment

Sea kayaks — 6 doubles	$21,000
Sea kayaks — 3 singles	7,500
Paddles — 15	3,000
PFDs (Pro) — 3	345
PFDs (regular) — 12	900
Spray decks — 15	2,250
Bailing pumps — 9	450
Dry bags — 15	150
Paddling jackets — 15	1,125
Boat trailer — 1	2,500
Tie-downs	100
Tents — 3	1,200
Stoves — 3	150
Pot sets — 3	100
Subtotal	**$40,770**

Office Equipment

Computer and software	$2,700
Desk	300
Chair	75
Misc. equipment	200
Subtotal	**$3,275**
Total start-up costs	**$44,045**

Loan Assumptions

Interest and principal payments over the term of the loan are calculated using a "present value table".

$$Payment = \frac{Note\ balance}{Table\ value}$$

————————— **$ 20,000 Note Payable, "A" at 10% interest for five years** —————————

$\dfrac{\$20{,}000}{\$3.7908} =$	$5,276	Yearly payment to D. Kitzman each year for 5 years

Principal	20,000	Payment breakdown, 1st year
Interest	6,380	$3,276 payment on principal
Total	**$26,380**	$2,000 payment of interest

————————— **$ 28,000 Note Payable, "B" at 14% interest for five years** —————————

$\dfrac{\$28{,}000}{\$3.4331} =$	$8,156	Yearly payment to bank each year for 5 years

Principal	28,000	Payment breakdown, 1st year
Interest	12,780	$4,236 payment on principal
Total	**$40,780**	**$3,920 payment of interest**

The size of the loan was determined based on the equipment start-up costs. Financial institutions will lend money against 60% of the net worth of the equipment ($28,000). For the rest of the required start-up cash, a loan of $20,000 will be obtained from David Kitzman, payable to him quarterly for five years at a rate of 10% interest.

Attachment A — Contractor Agreement

CONTRACT NO. _____

OWNER APPROVAL _____

THIS AGREEMENT, made on _____ (DATE)

BETWEEN: **"THE ADVENTURE COMPANY INC."**

(herein called the **"Company"**)

OF THE FIRST PART

AND: _____

_____

(herein called the **"Contractor"**)

OF THE SECOND PART,

WITNESSETH that the parties hereto agree as follows:

APPOINTMENT

1.   The Adventure Company retains the Contractor to provide the services (herein called the **"Services"**) described in Schedule "A" attached hereto and forming a part hereto.

TERM

2.   The Contractor shall provide the Services during the term of this Agreement (herein called the **"Term"**) which Term shall, notwithstanding the date of execution and delivery of this Agreement, be conclusively deemed to have commenced on the ____ st day of _____, 1998 and ending on the ____ st day of _____,1998.

PAYMENT

3.   The Adventure Company shall pay to the Contractor, in full payment for providing the Services and for expenses incurred in connection therewith, the amounts, in the manner and at the times set out in Schedule "B" attached hereto, and the Contractor shall accept the same as full payment as aforesaid.

INDEPENDENT CONTRACTOR

4.   The Contractor shall be an independent contractor and not the servant, employee or agent of The Adventure Company. The Contractor shall purchase and maintain adequate worker's compensation liability insurance.

5.   The Contractor shall not in any manner whatsoever commit or purport to commit The Adventure Company to the payment of any money to any person, firm or corporation.

6.   The Adventure Company may, from time to time, give such instruction to the Contractor as he considers necessary in connection with the provision of the Services but the Contractor shall not be subject to the control of The Adventure Company in respect of the manner in which such instructions are carried out.

7.   All employees of the Contractor providing services under this Agreement will remain at all times the employees or agents of the Contractor and not of The Adventure Company. Such employees are not entitled to and will not receive any benefits, allowances or rights in any way associated with persons having the status of employees or functioning as employees of The Adventure Company.

REPORTS

8.   The Contractor shall upon request, from time to time, of The Adventure Company, fully inform The Adventure Company of the work done and to be done by the Contractor in connection with the provision of the Services.

CONFIDENTIALITY

9.   The Contractor shall treat as confidential and shall not, without prior written consent of The Adventure Company, publish, release or disclose or permit to be published, released or disclosed, either before or after the expiration or sooner termination of this Agreement, any information supplied to, obtained by, or which comes to the knowledge of the Contractor as a result of this Agreement except insofar as such publication, release or disclosure is necessary to enable the Contractor to fulfil his obligations under this Agreement.

ASSIGNMENT AND SUBCONTRACTING

10.   The Contractor shall not without the prior written consent of The Adventure Company:

a)   assign, either directly or indirectly, this Agreement or any right of the Contractor under this Agreement; or

b)   subcontract any obligation of the Contractor under this Agreement.

11.   No subcontract entered into by the Contractor shall relieve the Contractor from any of his obligations under this Agreement or impose any obligations of liability upon The Adventure Company to any such subcontractor.

CONFLICT

12.   The Contractor shall not, during the Term, perform a service for or provide advice to any person, firm or corporation where the performance of the service or the provision of the advice may or does, in the reasonable opinion of The Adventure Company, give rise to a conflict of interest between the obligations of the Contractor to The Adventure Company under this Agreement and obligations of the contractor to such other person, firm or corporation.

INDEMNITY

13.   The Contractor shall indemnify and save harmless The Adventure Company from and against any and all losses, claims, damages, actions, causes of action, cost and expenses that The Adventure Company may sustain, incur, suffer or be put to by reason of any act or omission of the Contractor or of any servant, agent or subcontractor of the Contractor.

TERMINATION

14.   Notwithstanding any other provision of this Agreement, if the Contractor fails to comply with any provision of this Agreement then, and in addition to any other remedy or remedies available to The Adventure Company, The Adventure Company may, at its option, terminate this Agreement by giving written notice of termination to the Contractor.

15.   This Agreement may be terminated by the mutual agreement of both parties, signified by the exchange of letters executed by both parties, citing the date of termination agreed to and the arrangements agreed to for concluding the service.

16.   If the option described in paragraph 14 is exercised or if both parties agree to terminate the Agreement as described in paragraph 15, The Adventure Company shall be under no further obligation to the Contractor except to pay to the Contractor such amount as the Contractor may be entitled to receive, pursuant to Schedule "B" attached hereto, for Services provided and expenses incurred to the date the termination notice is given or delivered to the Contractor or agreed to by both parties.

NON-WAIVER

17.   No provision of this Agreement and no breach by the Contractor of any such provision shall be deemed to have been waived unless such a waiver is in writing signed by The Adventure Company.

18.   The written waiver by The Adventure Company of any breach of any provision of this Agreement by the Contractor shall not be deemed a waiver of such or of any subsequent breach of the same or any other provision of this Agreement.

APPROPRIATION

19.   Notwithstanding any other provision of this Agreement, the payment of money by The Adventure Company to the Contractor pursuant to this Agreement is subject to meeting the minimum requirements as identified in Schedule "B".

MISCELLANEOUS

20.   This Agreement shall be governed by and construed in accordance with the laws of the Province of British Columbia.

21.   The Schedules to this Agreement are an integral part of this Agreement as if set out in length in the body of the Agreement.

22.   In this Agreement wherever the singular or masculine is used it shall be construed as if the plural or feminine or neuter, as the case may be, had been used where the context or the parties hereto so require.

23.   The headings appearing in this Agreement have been inserted for reference and as matter of convenience and in no way define, limit or enlarge the scope of any provision of this Agreement.

IN WITNESS WHEREOF the parties hereto have executed this Agreement the day and year first above written.

THE ADVENTURE COMPANY: **CONTRACTOR:**

_____   _____
(Authorized Signature)   (Signature)

Index

B

balance sheets 50
barriers and profitability........................31
bottom-up budgeting 54
bottom-up pricing 89
break-even analysis 87
business mosaic 27
business plans 68
business plan example............................95

C

cash flow cycle...................................46
characteristics of tourism 80
contribution approach to pricing..............87
co-operative 39
corporation.......................................38
CPR...10
current asset management 46

D

definition, Ministry of Forests 16
definition, Tourism Growth Strategy 17
distribution channels 84

E

economic driver 10
entry barriers 32
exit barriers 32

F

financial analysis 55
general partnership 37

G

Gordonstoun 12
guiding and business efficiencies 24
guiding mosaic....................................25

I

income statements 50

L

limited partnership 37
long-term financing................................48

M

marketing expenditures 92
mission statement 74

N

non-profit society 39
Noyce, Wilfred....................................10
number of operators in B.C.........................17

O

operator stability.................................85
Outward Bound.....................................12

P

partnership agreement 40
positioning adventure products 80
pricing adventure products.......................86
pricing, bottom-up 89
product positioning maps..........................81
profit margins 90
pro forma balance sheets 51
pro forma income statements 51
proprietorship 36

R

ratio analysis 55
roots of commercial adventure.................10

S

short-term financing 47
size of the industry 15
stages of business growth
      development and survival 62
      expansion and maturity 64
      growth 63
      inception 62
starting a business 30
start-up action plans 74

T

tourism expenditures 16
tourism - personal growth -
      recreation cycle 13
tour operators 84
travel agents 84

W

wholesalers 84

Y

Yamnuska Inc. 13